Anonymous

The guide to and through Florida

Anonymous

The guide to and through Florida

ISBN/EAN: 9783337216672

Printed in Europe, USA, Canada, Australia, Japan

Cover: Foto ©Andreas Hilbeck / pixelio.de

More available books at **www.hansebooks.com**

Guide To and Through Florida,

"THE LAND OF FLOWERS,"

CONTAINING A

HISTORICAL SKETCH, GEOGRAPHICAL, AGRICULTURAL AND
CLIMATIC STATISTICS, ROUTES OF TRAVEL BY LAND
AND SEA, AND GENERAL INFORMATION

INVALUABLE TO THE

Invalid, Tourist or Emigrant.

Entered according to Act of Congress, in the year 1876, by
JONAH H. WHITE,
in the Office of the Librarian of Congress, at Washington.

GUIDE TO AND THROUGH FLORIDA.

HISTORIC SKETCH.

Five years after Christopher Columbus first saw land in the New World, another navigator, Sebastian Cabot, sailing under the English flag, discovered the coast of Florida. This was in 1497. It was not until the spring of 1512 that the Europeans made a permanent landing. A veteran cavalier of Spain, Juan Ponce de Leon, impelled by a romantic fancy that in the West there existed a fountain whose waters restored the aged to perpetual youth, raised an expedition of enthusiasts like himself and set sail on this wondrous voyage of discovery. He saw the coast for the first time on Easter Sunday, in April, 1512, which day the Spaniards call *Pasqua Florida,* and because the charming country spread before him was fairly radiant with wild flowers, he gave it the beautiful name of Florida. This landing was made near the site of the present city of St. Augustine.

The cavalier's search for the immortal spring was fruitless. The Indians harassed and picked off his band with poisoned arrows, and he was finally forced to quit the country. He carried with him to Cuba a mortal wound which caused his death soon after his arrival there. A dozen years later Spain again attempted to colonize the peninsula. Narvaez was appointed Governor and landed with three hundred men. He made no attempt at settlement however, but wandered off on an exploring expedition, and after many hardships, finally reached the far off country of the Mexicans. The illustrious Ferdinand de Soto, the discoverer of the Mississippi river, followed him to Florida. He landed in Tampa Bay with a thousand followers, in the spring of 1539. His march through the interior was disputed at every step by the aborigines, and his little army was so decimated by war, fatigue and sickness, that when his own body was committed to the bosom of the "Father of Waters" two years later, but a third of them survived.

The first actual settlement of Florida was made by the French Huguenots who, under Jean Ribault, attempted to plant a colony at the mouth of the St. Johns River in 1564. This roused the ire of the Spaniards, who claimed the country as their own, and an expedition was sent out under the command of Don Pedro Menendez to exterminate the Frenchmen. The Don did his bloody work effectually. The little French city was taken by surprise, and all of its inhabitants were massacred. Above their bodies, which he had suspended from the trees, Menendez left this inscription: "Not because they are Frenchmen, but because they are heretics and enemies of God." But vengeance on the cruel Castilians was swift. Three years later an expedition under De Gourgues, a Huguenot gentleman, set sail from France, and landing at St. Augustine, which the Spaniards had just built, attacked and took it after a severe battle. A portion of the garrison were taken to the site of the ruined French settlement on the St. Johns, and there hung to the same trees, with this inscription over their heads: "Not because they are Spaniards, but because they are traitors, robbers and murderers."

It was in 1565 that Menendez founded the city of St. Augustine, the oldest within the present limits of the United States. From this foothold colonies were sent out along the coast and into the interior of the province, and for an hundred years or more Florida was a growing and thriving Spanish colony. The Indians were almost uniformly hostile, but the superior civilization prevailed over them. Many vestiges of the early Spanish settlements in the State remain to show what the country was at this flourishing era of its history. The period of its decadence was at the conclusion of the great Continental war of 1753-60, when it passed from Spain into the possession of Great Britain. In the meantime it had been the scene of many conflicts. The English, under Sir Francis Drake, attacked and plundered St. Augustine in 1586. It was pillaged by the Indians in 1611, and sacked by the Buccaneers in 1665. Governor Moore, of South Carolina, raided into the colony in 1702, and unsuccessful attempts were made by the Georgians in 1725, 1740 and 1743 to capture and destroy St. Augustine.

In 1763 Spain ceded the whole territory of Florida to Great Britain. So greatly had its prosperity declined that its population did not exceed 600. In 1781, the Spaniards captured Pensacola, and three years later, by virtue of the treaty of 1784, they resumed jurisdiction over the country. During the last war with Great Britain the English troops under Col. Nichols occupied Pensacola, but General Jackson appearing before the town, they decamped to their fleet. Jackson, while fighting the Indians in 1818, was so affronted by the conduct of the Spanish governor that he took possession of Pensacola and sent the Spanish prisoners to Havana.

) The Spanish government recognized "manifest destiny" in 1819, and consented to the cession of the entire territory of Florida to the United States. The exchange of flags took place in 1821, a territorial government was established in 1822, and Florida was admitted as a State into the Union in 1845.

From the time of the cession down almost to our own day, there have raged those desolating Indian wars which reddened the border settlements with the blood of white men, women and children, and made the Everglades resound with the dying whoop of the hunted Seminole. The story of the valor of Coa-cou-chee, of Osceola, and of Little Cloud, fighting the last battles of their race for the hunting grounds of their ancestors, has passed into poetry and romance.

Florida, like her sister Southern States, was a battleground between North and South in the late civil war. After the passage of the ordinance of secession in 1861, Fort Pickens in Pensacola harbor, was invested by the Confederate troops, and the Navy Yard was occupied. Fernandina and St. Augustine were captured by Admiral Dupont's fleet in 1862. The following month the United States forces occupied Jacksonville, and the Confederate authorities abandoned nearly the whole of Northern and Western Florida, including Pensacola, and withdrew their army into Georgia. The year 1864 was characterized by raids on both sides. General Birney penetrated to Trent Creek, and the Confederate salt works at Ocala were destroyed. In February of this year General Trueman Seymour marched westward with a large body of United States troops, and at Olustee was disastrously defeated by the Confederate army under General Joseph Finegan. He retreated with a loss of 1200 men, leaving his dead and wounded on the field; and during the remaining months of the war the Federals were on the defensive.

After the surrender of General Lee, at Appomattox,

Virginia, the people of Florida abandoned further resistance, and the State was duly reconstructed by Congress.

GEOGRAPHY.

The State of Florida extends from the parallel of 31° North latitude to 25° North latitude, and lies within 80° and 88° West longitude from Greenwich. It is in the same latitude with the Desert of Sahara, Southern China and Northern Mexico, but its comparative degree of heat is not accurately indicated by its latitude, for it is isothermal with the Bermudas, Egypt, Northern Hindostan, Southern California and Louisiana. Moreover, lying between the Gulf of Mexico and the Gulf Stream, its main portion is fanned by ocean breezes which materially modify the temperature.

The shape of the State has been likened to that of a boot; the foot part being Northern Florida, and the leg being the peninsula. The first extends about 350 miles from East to West, and the peninsula 400 miles from North to South, and ninety miles, on the average, from East to West. The Gulf Stream skirts the Eastern coast about 300 miles. The State contains 59,868 square miles, or 37,931,520 acres, and is therefore a little larger than Georgia, Illinois or Michigan, and almost as large as the New England States or the united kingdoms of Portugal, Belgium and the Netherlands. The extent of her coast line is rather extraordinary. It is not less than 1,100 miles; a distance nearly equal to that from Portland, Maine, to Jacksonville, Florida, in a straight line.

\The surface of the eastern section of the State is generally level. ، In Western Florida it is rolling or hilly. The extreme southern part is covered with swamps. The coast is indented with thousands of bays and inlets formed by the jutting of the land, and by innumerable islands. The principal rivers are the Apalachicola, which has its source in the mountains of Upper Georgia; the beautiful Suwanee, in Middle Florida; the Withlacoochee, the Ocklawha and the Indian River, in Southern Florida. The great stream of the State, however, is the magnificent St. Johns, which rises in the Everglades, and winds northward a distance of four hundred miles until it empties into the Atlantic Ocean below Jacksonville.

The peninsula is filled with beautiful lakes, some of them being navigable for large steamers, and one of them, Lake Okeechobee, in the Everglades, being fully forty miles long and thirty miles wide. The lake scenery, in the neighborhood of the upper waters of the St. John, is unsurpassed in loveliness. Several of the larger bays on the coast deserve notice. Tampa Bay, Apalachee Bay and Pensacola Bay, are broad and deep enough to float navies. The State abounds in remarkable mineral springs. The Wakulla River rises about ten miles northwest of St. Marks from one of them. The water is moderately cold and highly impregnated with lime. From the big spring of Chipola bursts a furious river; Silver Spring, in Marion County, is a basin of surpassingly clear and deep water. The Sulphur Springs of the Suwanee are a curiosity, and enjoy a local reputation for curing rheumatism, dyspepsia and other kindred diseases. Springs of salt water are not uncommon in the interior.

Scientists say that the geological formation of Florida is of comparatively recent origin. The opinion of one of them, relative to the peninsula, is expressed in this language: "The whole peninsula has been formed by the successive growth of coral reefs added concentrically from

North to South to the first deposits, while the accumulation between these reefs has been a mixture of coral and fragments of shells, the coral prevailing in some parts, as in the regions of the Everglades, and in other portions, especially the Northern and Eastern, the shell." Agassiz assumes, of the lower half of the peninsula, "that if the growth be one foot in a century from a depth of seventy-five feet, and that each successive reef has added ten miles of extent southward, it would have required, on this computation, 135,000 years to have formed the southern half of the peninsula." The upper part of Florida is, of course, much older.

Palmetto Tree,

CLIMATE AND PRODUCTIONS.

Florida undoubtedly possesses the most equable and salubrious climate, all the year round, of any State in the Union. The thermometer seldom rises above 90° in the summer, nor falls below 30° in the winter. The summer may be said to be seven months long, but the heat is not intense. This is attributable in a great degree to the circumstance that the peninsula is fanned on the East by the Atlantic breezes, and on the West by those of the Gulf of Mexico, both of which can be sensibly felt in the middle of the State.

The winter in Florida resembles very much the season known in more northern latitudes as the "Indian Summer." The climate of Florida, however, has the additional advantage of being more dry and elastic. Rain falls rarely during the winter months. Five out of six days are bright and cloudless, and of the most agreeable temperature. In Southern Florida frost very rarely appears. Even as far north as the Suwanee River there are generally but two or three nights in a whole winter when ice as thick as a half dollar is found. A consequence of the evenness of the temperature is the very delightful salubrity of the nights in the sultriest season of the year, by which the body is refreshed, the sleep rendered sound, and the natural faculties are restored to vigor.

The following tables show the range of the thermometer throughout the year in Florida, and the evenness of the temperature as compared with that of given points in the Northern States.

GUIDE TO FLORIDA.

Observations made at Jacksonville during the six months ending April 30th, 1874; showing the highest and lowest ranges of the barometer and thermometer during each month, the total rainfall, the number of rainy days, and the prevailing wind. (Furnished by Richard McLaughlin, Esq.)

Month.	BAROMETER.		THERMOMETER.			Total Rainfall in inches.	No. of Rainy Days.	Prevail'g Wind.
	Highest	Lowest	Highest	Lowest	Mean.			
November, 1873	30.437	29.374	83	30	59	2.88	8	S W
December, "	30.480	29.643	79	32	56	3.38	7	N
January, 1874	30.653	29.810	77	35	55	.82	7	N
February, "	30.862	29.845	81	37	58	7.33	12	N E
March, "	30.335	29.761	87	37	66	2.13	7	S W
April, "	30.370	29.703	91	42	70	1.60	6	S W

It is proper to observe that there is a marked difference in the theometric range at Enterprise, two hundred miles south of Jacksonville, the temperature being much more even.

The following is a comparative table, showing the monthly and yearly mean of twenty years at St. Augustine, of thirty-one years at West Point, and of thirty five years at Fort Snelling, Minn. :

	Jan.	Feb.	Mar.	Apl.	May	Jun.	July	Aug	Sep.	Oct.	Nov.	Dec.	YEAR.
St. Augustine, Fla . . .	57.03	59.94	63.34	68.78	73.50	79.36	80.90	80.58	78.60	71.88	64.12	57.26	69.61
West Point, N. Y. .	28.28	28.80	37.63	48.70	59.82	68.41	73.75	71.83	64.31	53.04	42.23	31.98	50.73
Ft. Snelling, Minn. .	13.76	17.57	31.41	56.34	58.97	68.46	73.10	70.05	58.86	47.15	31 67	16.89	46.54

In Florida an extraordinary variety of valuable productions are successfully cultivated. Lying as it does partly within the temperate zone and partly within the semi-tropical regions, within its limits may be seen flourishing most of the vegetation familiar to the soil of the Middle and Western States, together with the fruits of the West Indies. At least one-fourth of the entire area of the State is south of the line of frost, and will grow successfully the orange, the lemon, the citron, the grape fruit, the banana, the pine-apple, and the cocoa-nut. Most of the tropical trees and shrubs grow spontaneously. Tobacco, sugar and hemp have been cultivated to some extent, and can be made very valuable productions if systematically treated. The yield of sugar is much more to the acre than in Louisiana. Cotton has hitherto been the leading staple. Indian corn has been largely raised, but not in sufficient quantities to supply the home demand. Within a few years the raising of early vegetables for the Northern trade has been commenced, with great success, on the St. Johns River, and along the railroads. Among the vegetables which are readily grown and bring remunerative prices, are tomatoes, cucumbers, melons, green peas, beans, cabbages, turnips, beets, squashes, onions, asparagus, and sweet and Irish potatoes. Wheat has been partially cultivated in the northern part of the State. The Ramie plant has just been introduced, and it is believed will become an important staple. Arrowroot, indigo, the castor bean, can be raised without difficulty. The large growth of the Mulberry renders the conditions favorable to the production of the silk worm. There is no reason why tea and coffee cannot be cultivated, as the climate and soil are especially adapted to the purpose. Of the fruits other than tropical, the peach, grape, fig, pomegranate and plum are produced. Berries grow profusely.

Florida is the best timbered State in the Union. Over 30,000,000 of acres are covered with heavy forests. The business of cutting and shipping lumber is large and increasing. Florida also exports naval stores, and at Key West there are extensive salt works. Further remarks on the soil and productiveness of the State will be found in the paragraphs devoted to the advantages of Florida for immigrants.

Population, Social and Political Condition.

According to the census of 1870 the population of Florida aggregates 187,748; of which 96,057 are whites and 91,689 blacks. This shows a proportion of a fraction over three inhabitants to the square mile; a density about equal to that of the States of Kansas and Texas. The population of the State in 1860 was 140,123, so that in spite of the ravages caused by the civil war, the increase in ten years has been 47,625, or thirty-four per cent.

The leading cities and towns in the State are Jacksonville with a population of 13,000, Fernandina with 2,500, Tallahassee with 2,500, St. Augustine with 2,000 Lake City with 2,000, Pensacola with 2,000, Gainesville with 1,500, Key West with 3,000; Palatka with 1,000, Quincy with 800, and Apalachicola with 1,000.

The seat of government is at Tallahassee. The new constitution, adopted by the people and approved by Congress in 1868, vests the executive power in a Governor, who is elected for four years. He is assisted in his deliberations by a Cabinet, composed of the principal officers in the State, viz: the Secretary of State, the Attorney-General, the Comptroller, the State Treasurer, the Surveyor-General, the Superintendent of Instruction and the Commissioner of Immigration. This is a novel feature in the framework of a State government, but was suggested by the success of the arrangement in the Federal system. The legislative power is vested in a Senate and Assembly. The former consists of twenty-four members, elected for four years; the latter of fifty-three members, elected for two years. The judicial power is vested in a Supreme Court, Circuit Courts, County Courts and Justices of the Peace. The Judges of the Supreme Court are appointed for life, of the Circuit Courts for eight years, and of the County Courts for four years. The election for State and County Officers and Members of the Legislature takes place the first Tuesday after the first Monday in November. Annual Sessions of the Legislature are held, beginning on the first Tuesday after the first Monday in January.

The present State government (1875–6) is as follows:

Governor,	M. L. STEARNS.
Lieutenant-Governor,	
Secretary of State,	S. B. McLIN.
Comptroller.	C. A. COWGILL.
Treasurer,	C. H. FOSTER.
Attorney-General,	WM. A. COCKE.
Commissioner of Immigration,	D. EAGAN.
Superintendent of Public Instruction,	J. C. GIBBS.

At the last Presidential election in the State (1872) the vote was as follows: Grant, 17,765; Greeley, 15,428; Republican majority, 2,337. The Republicans elected two majority in the State Senate, and three majority in the House of Representatives.

Florida, though one of the first-settled countries on this continent, has really all the characteristics of a new State,

Its scanty population has been scattered over a territory of nearly 60,000 square miles, and has heretofore been engaged almost wholly in agriculture. The social conveniences and advantages enjoyed in the thickly-settled States further North must not, therefore, be expected here. But immigration is pouring in and the State is rapidly improving. Schools and churches are to be found in all the towns and villages throughout the State, and a new system of public education has been provided for in the new constitution. In reference to the feeling of the old inhabitants towards new comers, the State Commissioner of Immigration, Mr. Adams, (himself a Northern man) writes:

"In our correspondence the question is often asked: 'Is it safe for a Northern man to come to Florida?' The answer is: That there is no sort of danger whatever. The immigrant of good character and habits will be readily received by all. Southern men and women are not super-human, and cannot be expected suddenly to absolve themselves from the domination of those trains of political thought and those prevalent social notions that have ruled them for years, or to sympathize at once with the political ideas of a triumphant radicalism. But the whole population of the State is becoming rapidly convinced that 'men, money and labor,' are to be watch-words in the success of the future of Florida. * * * Indeed, any good citizen that proposes to pay special attention to his own affairs, will be welcomed by all, and this without any sacrifice of principle or any abridgment of his rights of free thought and free speech. Northern men and women, who may come and persist in associating exclusively with each other, and sequester themselves diligently from all social intercourse with old residents, will be allowed thus to indulge their social predilections without let or hindrance."

Florida for Pleasure Seekers.

It has been well said that no part of the United States can furnish a more exciting and agreeable winter hunting-ground than Indian River and the Gulf Coast. Turkeys, Ducks, Squirrels, Deer and Bear are to be found throughout the State. The hunter in the Indian river region " may comfortably camp out, month after month, with a single blanket, taking as he needs his sweet potatoes from the ground, and the orange, lemon and banana from the plantations along the route, and in the continuous sunshine of an unending spring surfeit himself with the pursuit of game."

In the rivers and bays of Florida the lover of angling will find his real paradise. They literally swarm with valuable fish. Mullet, Bass, Sheepshead, Trout, Perch—salt water and fresh—and innumerable other varieties abound. The fish caught in the Lower St. Johns will run from one to forty pounds in weight. Lakes Harney and Jessup are abundantly stocked with fish of excellent quality, which are easily caught with nets, hooks or spears.

Alligator hunting is a sport peculiar to these southern latitudes and can be enjoyed to perfection along the rivers, lakes and lagoons of Florida. It takes a practiced eye to detect an alligator, for it closely resembles a rotten log, half-submerged and motionless. Shooting the alligator from the decks of the river steamers is a common enough custom, but the real alligator hunt is to be had on the upper lakes where they swarm in almost countless numbers. Hunting parties for Lake Harney are made up at Enterprise, on the Upper St. Johns. The expense is not much and the amusement prodigious.

Harper Bros. St. Augustine.

The antiquarian and enthusiast in historical research will find abundant material of interest in the visible traces of the Spanish occupation of two and three centuries ago. Remains of ancient cities, forts, breastworks, churches, and roads may be found, sometimes when least expected, in the midst of dense forests which have grown up and covered the vestiges of the early civilization. St. Augustine the oldest city on the North American continent, is unsurpassed in interest to the antiquarian. The battle fields of the later Indian wars also have a peculiar attractiveness. Here the tourist may study the historic spots illustrated by the valor and genius of Jackson, Taylor and Worth. The State of Florida offers rare opportunities for study to the students in Geology and Botany. The former have an interesting and important subject for investigation in the extraordinary coral formation of the peninsula; the latter in the wonderful and varied growth of floral and other vegetation. Several professors of Natural History from Northern institutions of learning were in Florida last year, collecting specimens of insects, birds, fishes and beasts. There are several excellent taxidermists in Savannah who make a business of preparing specimens for naturalists.

There are those to whom field and water sports are uninteresting. They travel for a love of change merely, or to behold the beautiful and novel in nature or to enjoy *idleness*—as a relaxation from severe and unremitting labor. The soft, balmy air, the clear, blue sky, the genial, though never enervating warmth, the tropical richness of the verdure, the bright-plumaged birds filling the forests with their music, the placid, transparent lakes and river scenery of unsurpassed loveliness, fulfil all the conditions required by this class of tourists. No American need seek an Italy across the waters when one lies here, almost within a day's travel.

FLORIDA FOR INVALIDS.

For more than a century Florida has been a resort for invalids from all parts of the world and particularly for those afflicted with pulmonary complaints. The dryness, evenness and salubrity of the climate are a most delightful and health-restoring change from the piercing winds and frigid temperature of the Northern, Middle and Western States in the winter. That many consumptives who have come to Florida die of the disease is true, but it is equally certain that they had postponed their visit until it was beyond the power of any climatic change to effect a cure. But there are thousands of persons threatened with the consumptive's death who have recovered their health in Florida, or at least have lengthened their days not unpleasantly.

It is estimated that at least forty thousand people visited Florida last winter, of whom about a fourth were invalids. The many beautiful villages and landings on the St. Johns River, as far up as Enterprise, were crowded with these seekers for renewed life and health. St. Augustine and the Indian river country, on the Atlantic coast, were also filled with visitors of the same character. Among these were not only people troubled with lung diseases, but those who were suffering from nervous complaints and from physical and mental prostration. Many were overworked business men from the great cities of the North and West, who sought this delicious and invigorating mode of recuperation.

The mildness of the atmosphere in winter permits much exercise in the open air. It is not uncommon for the native ladies to walk late in the moonlight evenings covered, as to the head, only with a lace veil. Some nights are damp and chilly, particularly in the Northern parts of the State, and a little fire is comfortable; but usually, throughout the winter, the inhabitants sit without a fire and with open doors and windows. These remarks are not intended to convey the idea that caution as to clothing can be neglected by the invalid. A writer on this point says: "As a rule, invalids should not expose themselves to the night air nor be tempted on warm, bright days to lay aside thick shoes and comfortable clothing. The invalid should always be clad in woolen clothing, and the robust do not require a linen suit except in the summer months."

Statistics testify to the healthfulness of Florida. Notwithstanding the fact that so many thousands of consumptives resort to the State for relief, the proportion of deaths from pulmonary complaints in it is less than in any other State in the Union.

The census of 1870 showed that these deaths were as follows:

Massachusetts,	one in 283
Maine,	" 315
Vermont,	" 463
New York,	" 379
Pennsylvania,	" 470
Ohio,	" 507
California,	" 450
Virginia,	" 585
Indiana,	" 599
Illinois,	" 698
Florida,	" 1,433

There is a wide-spread misapprehension respecting the malarial character of the interior of Florida. It is supposed that in some parts the air is charged with the most poisonous and noxious vapors arising from the swamp lands, and that fevers are common in consequence of it.

It is true that there is much swampy land in the State, and that wherever there is a dense vegetable growth accompanied by decomposition, malarious diseases arise, but in this case, the magnificent breezes, which sweep across the country, clear the atmosphere and purge it of its evil humors. All fevers in Florida assume a much milder type than in other sections where they are prevalent. Surgeon-General Lawson, of the United States Army, in his report explicitly asserts this. He says that statistics show "that the ratio of deaths to the number of cases of remittent fever has been much less among the troops serving there than in any other portion of the United States. In the Middle Division the proportion is 1 death to 36 cases of remittent fever; in the Northern Division, 1 to 52; in the Southern Division, 1 to 54; in Texas, 1 in 78; in California, 1 in 122; in New Mexico, 1 in 148; while in Florida it is 1 in 287.

The remedial character of the springs, which abound in every part of the State, must not be overlooked. Some are known to be highly beneficial to rheumatic and dyspeptic patients. A reference to the index of this work will give inquirers the location of several of the best esteemed spas in the State.

FLORIDA FOR IMMIGRANTS.

The Legislature of Florida has taken active measures to induce immigrants, from the North and West and from Europe, to settle in the State. A Department of Immigration has been established in connection with the State Government; the officer is styled Commissioner of Immigration, and he is a member of the Governor's Cabinet. The Bureau furnishes, upon application, all the information an intending settler may desire about the price, character and situation of lands and the means of getting to them.

It may be succinctly said that the inducements to immigration to Florida consist in the cheapness of the lands, ease of tillage, wide scope of crops, heavy profits and healthfulness of climate. The lands of the State are classified as swamp lands, high and low hummock and pine. The first are the most durably rich lands in the Union. Ditching is indispensable in preparing them for profitable cultivation; then they produce a succession of luxuriant crops with the most wonderful vigor. They are especially adapted for sugar, and have been known to yield four hogsheads to the acre, which is more than twice the average of Louisiana productiveness. There is at least a million of acres of this land vacant in Florida, most of which can be bought of the State for less than two dollars per acre.

The characteristic of the hammock, as distinguished from the pine land, is, that it is covered with a growth of underbrush, while the latter is open. Whenever the land is not so low as to be called a swamp and produces an undergrowth of shrubbery, it is called hammock. These lands stud the pine forests every few miles and vary in extent from twenty acres to forty thousand acres. The low hummocks require a little ditching, and are adapted to the growth of the cane. The high hummocks are composed of very rich soil and produce, with very little cultivation, all the crops of the country. They require no other preparation than clearing and ploughing, and are the lands most sought after by new settlers; the price varies from 25 cents to $25.00 per acre, according to location.

The pine lands are generally cleared by girdling the trees and cutting away the underbrush. The following year nothing remains but the trunks and dry branches which offer no further impediment to the rays of the sun. The fertility of what is denominated "first-rate pine" is remarkable. Some districts have yielded during fourteen years of successive cultivation, without the aid of manure, 400 pounds of Sea Island Cotton to the acre. The poorer classes of pine lands are valuable for the raising of Sisal hemp. They afford an excellent range for cattle, and are worth still more for their timber and naval stores. Prices of "first-rate pine" land varies from 25 cents to $10 per acre, according to location.

Unimproved lands on the St. Johns River can be had at from $5 to $15; and improved lands in the same locality at from $20 to $30. Plantations in other parts of the State, partially cleared and having some improvements, such as buildings and fences, are worth from $3 to $10 per acre. Lands, having orange groves in bearing, are from $50 to $250 per acre. On account of the genial climate, the finished, compactly-built dwelling-houses of the more rigorous North are not required. Less expensive buildings, the cost being not more than from $200 to $500, will answer every purpose of health and comfort.

The extraordinary variety of crops suitable to the soil of Florida is alluded to on another page. Many of them, with much less of the cost and hard labor expended in other farming sections of the Union, can be made exceedingly profitable. For settlers of small means the early vegetable cultivation and the raising of fruit make handsome returns, and for large capitalists there are fortunes in the production of cotton, sugar, fine Cuban tobacco and naval stores. There are also similar inducements in stock raising, the cutting of timber and lumber, salt making and the fisheries. Enterprising men and women, who know "how to keep a hotel," can settle anywhere along the railroad lines or on the St. Johns, and depend on constant and remunerative business.

Visitors to Florida, for the first time, are usually apprehensive about *snakes*. Notwithstanding its tropical situation there are few poisonous reptiles in Florida. In some localities the rattlesnake may be found, if sought for diligently, but generally the only snake visible is a species of harmless, water snake. The alligators are not aggressive towards strangers. They are rather disposed to run than fight when attacked. The mosquitoes flourish in the summer season, as they do everywhere else, but are less voracious than the Jersey breed. The other bugbear to the stranger in Florida—the malarial fever, is spoken of elsewhere. When it does occur, it is of the very mildest type, is not necessarily dangerous and yields easily to simple remedies.

Charleston, S. C.

Charleston, the principal city of South Carolina, and the largest on the Atlantic coast of the United States south of Baltimore, is situated on a tongue of land between the rivers Ashley and Cooper. Its population in 1870 was 48,956, of which 26,173 were negroes and mulattoes. It is a large cotton and rice mart, and is connected with the interior of the country by extensive lines of railway.

History—Charleston was originally settled by the English in 1679. It was one of the most important and opulent of the old colonial cities. In 1776 the British fleet, under Sir Peter Parker, was beaten off by the fort on Sullivan's Island. The city was captured by the British in 1780. The great civil war of 1860-65 began here with the passage of the ordinance of secession in December, 1860.

Harbor—The harbor is one of the largest and handsomest on the coast of America. The ruins of Fort Sumter, situated at its entrance, constitutes the spot of most interest to strangers visiting Charleston. Castle Pinckney, a short distance from the city, and Fort Moultrie, on Sullivan's Island, are also fortresses of historic renown. A packet yacht conveys visitors to these points every afternoon. Information of the hour of sailing, etc., may be obtained at the hotels.

Reminiscences.—Charleston possesses an unusual interest for visitors, as having been the birthplace of the Southern Confederacy, and the scene of some of its most stirring incidents. Its streets to this day abound with reminders of the momentous events which characterized its existence during that memorable four years struggle.

Streets—Meeting street is the longest and most elegant avenue. King street is the fashionable shopping thoroughfare. They run parallel the entire length of the city.

St. Michael's Church—This venerable edifice on the corner of Broad and Meeting street, is worth seeing. The chime of bells in its belfry were first imported from England about the middle of the last century; during the Confederacy were removed to Columbia for safety; at the close of the war were sent to England for re-casting, and in 1866 were returned, and once more rang out from the spire their merry peal to the air of "Home Again." From this steeple the Colonial troops kept watch upon the movements of the British, and later, the Confederate lookouts upon the Federal blockading squadron. The view which it affords of the city, the harbor and the back country is one which no tourist should miss.

Public Buildings—The Post Office building at the lower end of Broad street, is an ante-revolutionary structure. In its cellars American prisoners were cruelly incarcerated during the war for independence. The new Custom House is an imposing marble building. The Orphan House on Calhoun street is one of the architectural ornaments of the city. On its grounds is a marble statue of William Pitt, erected by the citizens of Charleston previous to the Revolution. The Charleston College, the Medical College, Roper's Hospital, the City Hall, Citadel, and the Arsenal, are large and handsome buildings. There is an interesting museum connected with the Charleston College.

Hotels—Those tourists who include a stop at Charleston in their Florida trip, either going or returning, will find the Charleston Hotel still deserving its well earned popularity.

During the summer of 1874 this famous house underwent a complete and expensive renovation. The proprietors have added to its many comfortable appointments the luxury of hot and cold water baths on each floor of the building, these baths being supplied at great expense with the celebrated Artesian water, famous for its many curative qualities.

One of the great attractions of the hotel is its superb double colonnade. During the past season the Post Band discoursed fine music from the balcony twice a week in the evenings.

Families desiring rooms can write or telegraph their requirements to the proprietors in advance, and so avoid disappointment.

The Pavilion Hotel, too, under the experienced proprietorship of Messrs. G. T. Alford & Co., deservedly receives a large share of tourists' patronage. Recently refitted and decorated throughout, and, offering in addition to the comforts of a home, the attractions of an unsurpassed *cuisine* and delightful verandahs, it ranks among the first hotels on the Atlantic Southern seaboard, and will be found everything that either the transient or permanent visitor could desire. Tourists can telegraph and secure rooms in advance.

Places worth Visiting—Pleasant trips may be made by the ferry-boats to Moultrieville and Mount Pleasant, the summer resorts of the Charlestonians. Those who prefer to sail or row around the historic waters of Charleston Harbor, will find a fine collection of boats for hire, on reasonable terms, at Capt. Young's wharf. Magnolia Cemetery, a short distance beyond the city lines, is a beautiful spot and has many fine monuments. The Battery, at the lower end of Meeting street, is a magnificent promenade and affords an excellent view of the harbor. The Burnt District, which extends from river to river across the middle of the city, marks the track of the great fire of 1864. The markets should be visited on a Saturday night, and some of the large Rice Mills are interesting. A trip to the wonderful Phosphate Grounds should not be omitted. At the Academy of Music, one of the most elegant theatres in the Union, operatic and dramatic performances are given during the winter.

The Suburbs of Charleston—There are many points of beauty and historic interest within easy distance of the city, and which no tourist should omit to visit. Prominent among these are the Drayton House, a splendid old baronial mansion of brick, redolent with traditions of the grandeur and hospitality it has witnessed in its past. It fronts upon the Ashley River, and is surrounded by a wealth of shrubbery and foliage. Magnolia Plantation and Schievelin, both also upon the same stream, are well worth visiting. A small steamer plies up the Ashley from Charleston for the accommodation of tourists.

The connecting at Savannah, of the Savannah & Charleston and Atlantic and Gulf Railroads, form an unbroken line from Charleston to Jacksonville, including all Eastern and Western points, via. Augusta (Port Royal R. R.) to Jacksonville, &c.

SAVANNAH, GA.

The commercial emporium of the Empire State of the South, is beautifully situated on the Savannah River, about 18 miles from its mouth. Savannah, next to New Orleans, is the largest port of shipment of cotton in the Southern States, and one of the largest in the world. It is advantageously placed, for a great thriving and increasing business. The Savannah River affording water communication with the Northern part of the State for 380 miles. The Atlantic and Gulf Railroad connects it with the rich and growing sections of Southern, Middle and Upper Georgia, and with Florida and the Gulf ports. The Georgia Central road running through Middle Georgia to Atlanta, and the Savannah and Charleston Railroad to Charleston S. C., are important links connecting the city with the West and North. There are two lines of first-class steamers to New York, and weekly lines to Baltimore, Philadelphia and Boston.

Savannah, according to the census of 1870, had a population of 28,235, of which 13,068 were colored. Its receipts of cotton in 1872-3 amounted to 626,768 bales. It also exported 34,000,000 feet of lumber, and the total value of its exports that year was $50,000,000, which gave it the rank of the third exporting port in the United States. The city is handsomely laid out with broad streets closely shaded by water oaks, live oaks, magnolia, sycamore and pride of India trees. At nearly every other corner there is a public square, planted with these magnificent shade trees. The number of these squares is 24. South, Broad and Bay streets have grassy promenades in the middle, with carriage ways on either side.

History—Savannah was first settled in 1733 by Genl. Oglethorpe and about thirty families. Here, three years later, John Wesley preached for the first time in America. In 1766 there were four hundred dwellings here. In 1788 the British captured the city. Nearly a year later the brave Pulaski fell in a vain attempt by the combined French and American forces to recapture it. The British held possession till the war ended. In 1791 Washington, and in 1825, Lafayette visited Savannah. It was prominent during the Confederate war as the terminus of Genl. Sherman's celebrated "March to the Sea."

Public Buildings—There are many fine buildings in Savannah, among which may be mentioned the City Exchange, New Market House, St. Andrews Hall, the New Custom House and the Hall of the Georgia Historical Society. The Independent Presbyterian Church, the Masonic Temple, and St. John's Episcopal Church have considerable architectural merits. Greene Monument in Johnson square, and the Pulaski Monument in Monterey square should also be seen by visitors.

Suburban Points—Strangers will find many spots in and about Savannah worth visiting. *Fort Pulaski*, a few miles down the river, was the scene of a long siege during the late war. The original cost of its construction was $988,859. Daufuskie Island, near by, is memorable as the scene of the Bloody Point massacre of Indians by white settlers. Beach Hammock, Greenwich Park and Jasper Springs are also noted resorts within a few miles of the city.

Hotels—The Screven and Marshall Houses continue to furnish the best of accommodations, and at most reasonable prices, to tourists stopping in Savannah.

The Planters' and O'Connel's European House are also included in the list of Hotels.

Forsyth Park, though small in area (20 acres), is quite a resort for the citizens and attractive to strangers, as it is composed mostly of the natural growth of the forests. The fountain in the centre is considered a beautiful model. It is after the style of the fountains in the Place de la Concord in Paris. The walks are prettily laid out, and covered with shell. It is the fashionable resort for the elite of the city. In the rear of the Park, in a large enclosure known as the Parade Ground, stands the Confederate Monument, recently erected by the Ladies' Memorial Association, and which in point of beauty of design and finish, compares favorably with any in the South, and will cost when completed $25,000. In this spot, with its surrounding luxuriance of shrubbery and vegetation, the tourist will find much to charm and please the eye.

Bonaventure Cemetery, one of the loveliest spots in the world, has rural charms peculiar to itself. The long avenues, by the side of which the dead are sleeping are arched by the branches of great trees from which the gray moss sweeps in heavy festoons. There are some noticeable monuments in this cemetery, which derives its name from the original tract of which it formed a part, and which was first settled in or about 1670 by Col. John Mulryne, an Englishman. By the marriage of his daughter Mary in 1761 to Josiah Tatnall of Charleston, it came into possession of the latter family, and Gov. Tatnall of Georgia was born there in 1765. This marriage is of especial interest, as having, it is said, been the occasion of the planting of the great live oaks which now grace the spot. Tradition has it that they were planted in the forms of the letters M and T—the initials of the bride's and groom's respective family names.

In 1847 the estate passed into the hands of a Capt. P. Wiltberger, and was by him adapted to its present use. His remains now rest within its limits.

Thunderbolt, a picturesque bluff, 8 miles from the city, from which a good view of the country can be obtained, is a favorite resort for pleasure parties.

Monuments. A monument in honor of General Nathaniel Greene adorns Johnson Square. One to the memory of Count Pulaski is erected on the spot where he fell in the attack on the city in 1779.

The Theatre is open during the winter season and presents the best musical and dramatic artists of the country in succession.

Savannah enjoys an enviable reputation for salubrity. During the winter months the hotels and private boarding houses are filled with Northern visitors. The climate is better suited to some invalids than points further South. Tourists bound to Florida usually sojourn a few days in Savannah to enjoy its genial weather and visit its places of interest.

Points of Prominence in Florida and Southern Georgia, on the Line of the Atlantic and Gulf Railroad.

This Railroad is the great connecting link between the Atlantic coast railroads from the North (via Savannah) and Southern Georgia and Florida. It affords a through railroad connection for passengers and freight between those flourishing sections and Baltimore, Philadelphia, New York and Boston.

The main trunk extends from Savannah to Bainbridge, on the Flint River, nearly to the Alabama State line, a distance of 236 miles. There are two branch roads; one beginning at Du Pont and extending to Live Oak, a distance of forty-eight miles, and connecting with the Jacksonville, Pensacola and Mobile Railroad; and the other from Thomasville to Albany, Ga., a distance of fifty-eight miles. The Atlantic and Gulf Railroad also connects at Jesup with the Macon and Brunswick R. R., and at Way Cross with the Brunswick and Albany R. R.; passengers and freight are taken either for the coast, or for all points in Middle and Upper Georgia and Alabama.

———◆◆◆———

The following are the stations on the Atlantic and Gulf Railroad after leaving Savannah:

Ways—15¾ miles from Savannah, 220¼ miles from Bainbridge. Wood station. There are Presbyterian and Baptist Churches near here. The County seat of Bryan County is near here. Within one mile east of this station the road crosses the Great Ogeechee River. Some of the largest rice plantations in Georgia are situated on its banks. A short distance below the bridge the blockade runner, "Rattlesnake," previously the "Nashville," was sunk by the guns of the Federal fleet, then lying below Genesis Point. On this point was the Confederate battery, Fort McAllister, which was captured after a sharp fight, by Sherman's Army, on its "march to the sea."

Fleming—24 miles from Savannah and 212 miles from Bainbridge. Telegraph office. About fifteen miles from here, on the shore, is the harbor of Sunbury, one of the best on the Georgia coast, and one of the earliest settlements in the State. Visitors may see there the old Sunbury Fort and have a fine view of St. Catherine's Sound. At Fleming are Methodist and Baptist Churches.

McIntosh—32 miles from Savannah and 204 miles from Bainbridge. This station is two and one-half miles from the village of Flemington, Liberty County; five miles from Hinesville, the County seat; and ten miles from Riceboro, the head of water navigation on the North Newport River.

Walthourville—39 miles from Savannah, 197 miles from Bainbridge. The village of Walthourville is two miles from the station, and in ante bellum days was the summer residence of the wealthy planters of Liberty County. It was the birth-place of a number of the most eminent men of the State, and was noted for the intelligence and refinement of its society. Present population, 300. The place is a resort for invalids. There are good boarding houses kept by Messrs. Brown and Miller. Rates from $1.50 to $2.00 per day for transient visitors. The neighborhood abounds with deer and partridge. There are two churches in Walthourville, one Presbyterian and one Baptist.

Johnston—46 miles from Savannah, 190 miles from Bainbridge. Population, 150. The village contains a boarding-house, kept by Mrs. Johnston, two saw mills and a shingle mill near by. Plenty of game will be found in the vicinity.

Upon leaving this station, the road descends into the

valley of the Altamaha River. This river is one of the largest in the State and is formed by the junction of the Oconee and Ocmulgee Rivers; the former, navigable for steamboats to Dublin, and the latter to Macon. Darien, where a large trade is carried on in lumber and timber, lies near the mouth of the Altamaha. The Atlantic and Gulf Railroad crosses this stream upon a substantial lattice bridge of four spans, formed upon brick pieces of sufficient height for steamers to pass below. The swamp abounds in cypress and oak. The cypress is manufactured into shingles, and shipped to Macon, Savannah and Northern ports, and quantities of oak staves are exported to France and Spain.

Doctortown—53 miles from Savannah, 183 miles from Bainbridge. This station is near the site of an old Indian town, which was the abode of a famous "medicine man," whence the name of the station.

Jesup—57 miles from Savannah, 179 miles from Bainbridge. Telegraph office. Junction of the Macon and Brunswick Railroad. Passengers take cars here for Macon, Atlanta, and all points in Middle and Northern Georgia, Alabama and Tennessee. Connection is also made here with the growing and prosperous city of Brunswick, forty miles distant on the Atlantic coast. Population of Jesup, 600. The new hotel—the Altamaha—will accommodate 100 guests, has been fitted up with every comfort, and is well kept. It is the eating-house for both roads. The Wayne *Triumph* (weekly) is published here.

Screven—68 miles from Savannah, 168 miles from Bainbridge. Wood station.

Upon the line of the road for the thirty miles west of this station, in the finest lumber region of the State, are situated eight or ten large circular saw mills. The lumber interest is annually increasing in importance, and adds largely to the revenues of this road. The shipments of lumber over the road have increased from 8,000,000 feet in 1866, to 32,000,000 feet in 1871. Short lateral branches are being constructed into the virgin forests on either side of the line, and it is probable that the annual shipments will continue to increase for many years to come.

Patterson—77 miles from Savannah, 159 miles from Bainbridge. There are three churches in the vicinity.

Blackshear—86 miles from Savannah, 150 miles from Bainbridge. Population, 800. County seat of Pierce County. There are in the village and vicinity four saw mills and a grist mill. The Knoles House (Mrs. Way) accommodates travelers at $2.50 per day or $7.00 per week. The country hereabouts is heavily timbered, and large quantities of round and square timber are cut and shipped. There is a Methodist Church in the village.

Way Cross—96 miles from Savannah, 140 miles from Bainbridge—Junction of the Brunswick and Albany R. R.—57 miles from Brunswick. Population 600. County seat of Ware County. The town, which was laid out in 1872, stands on a sandy ridge, with a clay sub-soil, and a clear, bold stream of running water on the south. There is a commodious hotel (board $2.00 per day or $30.00 per month), a fine Church (Methodist), a neat Academy and a number of beautiful residences.

Tebeauville—97 miles from Savannah, 139 miles from Bainbridge. Telegraph office. Population about 100. Situated near the head of the great Okafonokee Swamp, which abounds with game and fish, and is a famous resort of the sportsman. The Railroad House at this station, kept by J. W. Remshart, will accommodate about thirty guests at $2.00 per day.

Homersville—122 miles from Savannah, 114 miles from Bainbridge. Population, 200. County seat of Clinch County. The Okafonokee Swamp is near by. Cowart's Hotel and Hodge's boarding house afford good accommodations to visitors and sportsmen. Sugar cane is raised to some extent on the neighboring plantations.

Du Pont—131 miles from Savannah, 105 miles from Bainbridge. Telegraph office. Junction with the Florida branch of the Atlantic and Gulf Railroad, (which see, at the end of this article.) The Railroad House accommodates travelers at $2.00 per day. In the village the Primitive Baptists have a small meeting-house. The climate here is agreeable and the water excellent. The country is heavily covered with yellow pine.

Stockton—139 miles from Savannah, 105 miles from Bainbridge. Wood station.

Naylor—144 miles from Savannah, 97 miles from Bainbridge. Population, about 75. There are two saw mills and a wool-carding establishment near here.

Valdosta—157 miles from Savannah, 79 miles from Bainbridge. Telegraph office. Population, 2000. County seat of Lowndes County. The largest town on the railroad between Savannah and Thomasville. It ships about 5000 bales of cotton per season, and contains several mills, five white and two negro Churches, and two good hotels, Stuart's Railroad Hotel and Tranquil Hall, where accommodations may be had at $5.00 per week for permanent guests. The *South Georgia Times* is published here. In the neighborhood are many natural curiosities; one of the small rivers enters a cave and disappears. Ocean Pond and Long Pond, from three to five miles in extent, afford the best fresh-water fishing in Georgia.

From this station westward to Thomasville, the road

passes through a region which, perhaps, offers more inducements to emigration than any other part of Southern Georgia or Florida. It is a rolling country, well watered. and thickly wooded with yellow pine and other timber, There are many thrifty farmers engaged in planting cotton, corn and sugar cane, and in raising stock for the Savannah market. In summer the southerly winds are cooled in passing over the Gulf of Mexico, and the nights are always pleasant. Cases of malarial disease are rare, and mosquitoes are almost unknown. In short, there is no other part of the Southern country possessing the same advantages of climate, soil and productions, of health, proximity to schools, churches and centres of trade, where land can be purchased at as small a price as in this vicinity. The Atlantic and Gulf Railroad was only extended to Thomasville at the beginning of the late war, and as it is not on any of the great Southern Through Lines, it has in a great measure escaped the attention of persons going South in pursuit of health or seeking a home.

Ousley—166 miles from Savannah, 70 miles from Bainbridge. Population, 150. Travelers are accommodated by J. A. and W. H. Ousley. In the vicinity are several pretty lakes.

Two miles west of this station the road crosses the Withlacoochee River, an affluent of the Suwanee. Upon its banks and near the road are two springs (one of them a sulphur spring), which enjoy quite a local reputation.

Quitman—174 miles from Savannah, 62 miles from Bainbridge. Telegraph office. One of the most flourishing towns in Southern Georgia. Population, 1500. County seat of the fertile county of Brooks, which contains ten water and six steam mills. In Quitman are two carriage manufactories, a cotton and wool factory with a capital of $75,000; five churches, belonging to the Methodists,

Baptists and Presbyterians; thirty business houses, mostly built of brick, and three educational institutions; the Lovick Pierce College with 60 students, Quitman Academy with 100 students, and the Howard Institute (colored) with 60 students. This young town was planned and the streets blazed out of the pine forests in 1860. Two weekly papers, *Gallaher's Independent* and the *Quitman Reporter*, both well conducted sheets, are published here. In the county is a partially explored cave, called the Devil's Hopper, which is a great natural curiosity. The sulphur springs are four miles distant from the town. Travelers are accommodated at the City Hotel (D. U. McNeil). and McIntosh House (J. R. Edmonson). Rates $2.00 per day.

Dixie—181 miles from Savannah, 55 miles from Bainbridge. Bryan's Hotel has good accommodations at $1.50 per day. Near by is Dry Lake, a large and beautiful sheet of water, and a sink hole into which three rivers empty and show no outlet again.

Boston—188 miles from Savannah, 48 miles from Bainbridge. Population, 400. Ships 1800 bales of cotton. Several steam saw mills here, and Methodist, Baptist and Presbyterian churches. Boston is the proposed terminus of two new railroads; one to St. Marys, Georgia, and the other to Greenfield, Georgia, and is growing rapidly.

Thomasville—200 miles from Savannah, 36 miles from Bainbridge. Telegraph office. Junction with Albany branch of the Atlantic and Gulf Railroad, (which see, at the end of this article.) Population, 4000. County seat of Thomas County. The town is situated on the highest land between Savannah and the Flint River, and is 97 feet higher than Albany. It is the centre of a thriving trade and bids fair to become the most important town in Southern Georgia. Its location is dry and healthy, and it is therefore a favorite resort for Northern invalids. The streets are broad and beautifully shaded with evergreens. The town has Episcopal, Methodist, Baptist, Presbyterian and Roman Catholic churches; five saw mills, a foundry and a tannery, and two newspapers, the *Southern Enterprise* and *Thomasville Times.* The South Georgia Agricultural and Mechanical Association holds its annual fairs here, generally continuing five days. The country around is cultivated with cotton and sugar, and is well settled. Travelers and invalids will find accommodations at the Gulf Railroad House, kept by G. W. Parnell, and Young's Hotel, by John McKinnon; charges $3.00 per day or $12.00 per week. At the boarding houses rates are from $20.00 to $25.00 per month. A Swiss Colony is successfully engaged in the grape culture near Thomasville. Thomasville shipped about 12,000 bales of cotton last year.

Cairo—214 miles from Savannah, 22 miles from Bainbridge. Population 66. Boarding houses kept by W. T. Rigsby, William Powell and Wily Pearce. Rates $1.00 per day.

Whigham—221 miles from Savannah, 15 miles from Bainbridge. A considerable trade done here with the surrounding country.

Climax—228 miles from Savannah, 8 miles from Bainbridge. Wood station. At this station the road descends westward into the valley of the Flint River.

Bainbridge—236 miles from Savannah. The Western terminus of the Atlantic and Gulf Railroad. Telegraph office, and the head of navigation on the Flint River, which is navigable all the year. Steamboats make semi-weekly trips to Columbus, Georgia, on the Chattahoochee and Apalachicola, Florida, on the Gulf of Mexico. The population of Bainbridge is 2000. It contains a cotton factory, two steam saw mills, and three churches. Two newspapers, the *Southern Sun* and the *Argus* are printed here. The neighboring lakes abound with fresh-water fish. The Sharon House, kept by John Sharon, is a first-class country house. Board $3.00 per day, $15.00 per week.

Bainbridge is the county seat of Decatur County. The local shipments of cotton are 11,000 bales. The steamers landing here bring about 16,000 bales per annum for shipment by rail to Savannah. The town is rapidly improving. It is also the terminus of the Bainbridge, Cuthbert and Columbus Railroad, (narrow gauge) now under construction.

Florida Branch of the Atlantic and Gulf Railroad.

From Du Pont, Georgia, to Live Oak, Florida.

Du Pont—131 miles from Savannah, 132 miles from Jacksonville. The junction of the main trunk of the Atlantic and Gulf Railroad and the Florida Branch.

Forrest—143 miles from Savannah, 121 miles from Jacksonville. Wood station.

Statenville—151 miles from Savannah, 111 miles from Jacksonville. Population, about 50. The place contains Baptist and Methodist churches.

Jasper—163 miles from Savannah, 99 miles from Jacksonville. Population, 150. County seat of Jasper County. Invalids take conveyances here for the Upper White Sulphur Springs, 18 miles distant. The country hereabout is pleasant and healthy. Visitors to Jasper can be accommodated at the Stewart House, kept by Judge H. J. Stewart, and the Hately House, by Mrs. Z. Hately. Charges, $15.00 to $20.00 per month, $2.00 per day.

Suwanee—171 miles from Savannah, 90 miles from Jacksonville. Wood station. About one mile from his station is a most remarkable Sulphur spring, upon the rocky shore of the widely-sung "Suwanee Ribber," and embowered in the live-oak and magnolia trees which shade its placid surface. The spring is about fifteen feet deep and as many feet in diameter; its crystal-pure waters, as they pour into the river, are so clearly separate from the dark current flowing down from the Okafonokee Swamp, that the line of demarkation may be observed for some distance below the spring. This spring is well known for its efficiency in cases of rheumatism and dyspepsia, as is also the Upper White Sulphur, some miles farther up the river.

Live Oak—179 miles from Savannah, 83 miles from Jacksonville. Telegraph office. Junction with the Jacksonville, Pensacola and Mobile Railroad.

Albany Branch of the Atlantic and Gulf Railroad.

From Thomasville to Albany, Georgia.

Thomasville—200 miles from Savannah, 60 miles from Albany. Junction of the main trunk and the Albany Division of the Atlantic and Gulf Railroad.

Okloknee—211 miles from Savannah, 49 miles from Albany.

Pelham—224 miles from Savannah, 36 miles from Albany.

Camilla—232 miles from Savannah, 28 miles from Albany. Telegraph office. A new town, laid out in 1857, and growing rapidly. Population, 500. Ships 5000 bales of cotton. It is situated in the midst of a flourishing cotton region. The town contains several steam saw mills, two corn mills, Methodist, Baptist and Presbyterian churches, two good hotels and a number of boarding houses. Prices at the former, per day $2.00 to $2.50; per week, $5.00 to $6 00. County seat of Mitchell County. From this station to Albany the road runs near the east bank of the Flint River, and through an almost continuous belt of extensive and fertile cotton plantations.

Baconton—242 miles from Savannah, 18 miles from Albany.

Hardaway—252 miles from Savannah, 8 miles from Albany.

Albany—Telegraph Office, 258 miles from Savannah and on the Flint River. The terminus of three railroads, the Albany Branch of the Atlantic and Gulf Railroad, the Brunswick and Albany Railroad to the Atlantic coast, and the South-western Railroad to Macon. Population, 3500. County seat of Dougherty County. This is also a new place and has risen to the dignity of an incorporated city. It contains a number of mills and foundries, seven churches, two newspapers, the *News* and *Central City*, and two hotels: the Central Hotel, kept by S. Atkinson, and the Albany House by M. Burnes. Rates $3.00 per day and $30.00 per month. Upland cotton is the staple product of the surrounding country. Blue Spring, three miles from Albany, is a bold stream, gushing from the earth, and abounding with fish. The many ponds in the county are supposed to have an underground connection with this spring.

NORTHERN FLORIDA.

From Quincy, via Live Oak, to Jacksonville, by the Jacksonville, Pensacola and Mobile Railroad.

The Jacksonville, Pensacola and Mobile Railroad connects the Apalachicola River in Western Florida with the Atlantic Ocean at Jacksonville, and therefore traverses the entire Northern section of the State, east of the Apalachicola. It also connects at Live Oak with the Atlantic and Gulf Railroad, and all stations in Georgia; at Tallahassee with St. Marks and the Gulf of Mexico, and at Baldwin with Fernandina in the North and Cedar Keys in the South. At present the road is in running condition from Quincy east to Jacksonville, a distance of 189 miles. The road will be completed this winter to Chattahoochee, and the work of making the connection with Pensacola and Mobile will be pushed forward rapidly.

The following are the stations on this road, going east:

Quincy—189 miles from Jacksonville. Telegraph office. Population, 800. County seat of Gadsden County. The Willard House, kept by Mrs. Willard, is recommended. Board, $3.00 per day. There is a boarding-house kept by Mrs. Innes. Quincy has three churches: Methodist, Episcopal and Presbyterian. A weekly newspaper, the *Quincy Journal*, is published here. The village is situated in Gadsden County, which before the war cultivated fine Cuba tobacco on a large and remunerative scale. The early vegetable business is flourishing. The neighborhood of Mount Pleasant, 12 miles from Quincy, is engaged in the cultivation of the Scuppernong grape, and produces a wine equal to the best of the Caliiornia and Ohio vintages. A number of Swedish immigrants have settled in Gadsden County, and have done so well that a large party has been iuduced to join them. Quincy is 22 miles from Bainbridge, Georgia, and with it has daily stage communication.

Tallahassee—24 miles from Quincy, 165 from Jacksonville (Telegraph office). Population 2,500. State capital and Leon county seat. The city is healthfully located upon the summit of a short ridge in the centre of a fine farming country, containing some of the best rolling lands in the State. Leon county raises about 12,000 bales of cotton annually. The climate is delightful, the summer heat being tempered by Gulf breezes. In the neighborhood of the city are Lakes Bradford, Jackson and Lafayette, all picturesque and beautiful bodies of water, and only sixteen miles distant are the celebrated Wakulla Springs, through the crystal waters of which one can plainly discern objects on the bottom, 130 feet below. Tallahassee boasts two newspapers, the *Floridian* and the *Sentinel*, a well kept hotel (the City) accommodating 150 guests, and kept by Mr. W. P. Slusser (board $3 per day), and in addition to the State House, numerous neat and tasteful edifices, public and private. During the past year, too, a grand impetus has been given to its manufacturing industries. A cotton mill, established by the Tallahassee Manf'g Co., is in active and prosperous operation, and the car shops of the J. P. & M. R. R. employ numerous hands in the construction of baggage, mail and express cars, containing all modern improvements. Emigration from the North in this section of Florida has of late begun to assume surprising dimensions, several large colonies having already settled or purchased in the immediate vicinity. For Northern Florida in general, and Tallahassee in particular, a new era of prosperity seems now to be dawning.

Monticello Junction—51 miles from Quincy, 138 miles from Jacksonville. Connection is had here with the town of Monticello, county seat of Jefferson County, which is the terminus of a branch road, four and a quarter miles distant. The population of Monticello is about 2000. Telegraph office. The Monticello *Advertiser* is published here, and there are Episcopalian, Methodist, Baptist and Presbyterian churches. The principal hotel is the Monticello, with good accommodations, and kept by Mrs. M. A. Madden. Board and lodging may be had for $25.00 per month. Lake Miccosukie is in this vicinity. Its banks are famous in the ancient history of Florida, as the camping ground of De Soto; and in modern history, as the field of a sanguinary battle between General Jackson and the Miccosukie tribe of Indians.

Monticello is twenty miles distant from Dixie, on the Atlantic and Gulf Railroad.

Aucilla—58 miles from Quincy and 131 miles from Jacksonville.

Goodman—65 miles from Quincy and 124 miles from Jacksonville. These two stations are shipping points for a fine planting country.

Madison—79 miles from Quincy and 110 miles from Jacksonville. Telegraph office. Population between 700 and 800. County seat of Madison County. The village contains Methodist, Baptist and Presbyterian churches. The lands hereabouts are good, and there is considerable early garden truck raised for the Northern markets. The Phœnix Mills in the village are of large capacity. Travelers can be accommodated at the house of Mr. W. E. Howells, at $2.50 per day. In the County of Madison the beautiful Lakes Rachel and Mary Frances, and Cherry Lake are situated. They abound with fish.

Ellaville—94 miles from Quincy and 95 miles from Jacksonville. An extensive lumbering place; situated on the Suwanee River, which empties into the Gulf of Mexico. Population, about 500. There are large saw mills at this place, whose cutting capacity is fifty thousand feet daily, also planing and grist mills. A boarding house in the village is kept by Mrs. Drew. The church is used by all denominations.

Live Oak—107 miles from Quincy and 82 miles from Jacksonville. The junction with the Atlantic and Gulf Railroad to Savannah, and all railroad points North. Telegraph office. County seat of Suwanee County. Population, 800. The village contains a saw mill, a planing mill, a manufactory and a church, which is used alternately by the Episcopalians, Baptists, Methodists and Presbyterians. The *Live Oak Herald* is published here. Conner's Hotel affords good accommodations. Fare, $3.00 per diem. There is a private boarding house kept by Mrs. McLarran. Near the village are many waterfalls, some of them very pretty. The site of Live Oak was once an Indian camping ground. The *Live Oak Times* is published here.

Wellborn—119 miles from Quincy and 71 miles from Jacksonville. Passengers going to White Sulphur Springs stop here. Population, 350. Wellborn is situated on the highest point above the level of the Gulf, on this railroad. It is in a healthy country and a resort for invalids. The celebrated White Sulphur Springs on the Suwanee River, are eight miles distant. They are much used by sufferers from dyspepsia and rheumatism. Lake Wellborn and several other inland sheets of water, are in this neighborhood, and are well stocked with fish. The village contains two churches, one used by the Baptists, and the other by the Methodists and Presbyterians. Travelers and invalids are accommodated at the houses of H.

D. Rigsbee, S. L. Williams and others. Rates, $1.50 daily, $7.00 to $8.00 weekly, $20.00 to $30.00 monthly.

Lake City—130 miles from Quincy and 59 miles from Jacksonville. Telegraph office. A city of 2000 inhabitants. An United States signal service station and the seat of justice of Columbia County. The place contains cotton, saw and grist mills; and seven churches belonging to the Roman Catholic, Presbyterian, Methodist, Episcopalian and Baptist denominations. The *Lake City Press*, edited by Captain E. W. Davis, is published here. Lakes Isabella, De Soto and Hamburg are within the city limits, and Indian Lake within a quarter of a mile. There is a chalybeate (iron, sulphur and magnesia) spring, about half a mile from the city, and one of the best sulphur springs in the South within 12 miles. The lakes and streams are stocked with trout, bream, perch, (mawmouth, speckled, sand and mud) gar and other varieties of fish; and the surrounding country with deer, bears, wild turkeys, partridges, snipe, (English and gray) and wild ducks. Every planter has from one to two dozen orange trees. The dim remains may be seen, about half a mile from Lake City, of trenches built by De Soto in his conflicts with the Indians over three hundred years ago. The city has three hotels, the Cathey House by J. W. Cathey, Hancock House by Mrs. Ashurst, and Thrasher House by T. B. Thrasher, each containing from 25 to 30 rooms.

Olustee—142 miles from Quincy and 47 miles from Jacksonville. Olustee is the site of the most important battle fought in Florida during the late civil war. Major General Trueman Seymour, with a large body of United States troops, in February, 1864, marched from Jacksonville, westward, and at this place encountered the Confederate army under Brigadier-General Joseph Finegan. A desperate battle ensued, which lasted all day, and was characterized by great bravery on both sides. General Seymour was beaten, and retreated from the field, abandoning his dead and wounded to the enemy. His loss was 1200, including Colonel Fribley, of the negro troops, killed. Finegans's loss was 250. The Confederate cavalry pursued General Seymour as far as Baldwin, picking up many prisoners.

Sanderson—152 miles from Quincy and 37 miles from Jacksonville. Telegraph Office. County seat of Baker County.

Baldwin—170 miles from Quincy and 19 miles from Jacksonville. Telegraph Office. Junction with the Florida Railroad, connecting with Fernandina and the Atlantic Ocean on the north, and Cedar Keys and the Gulf of Mexico, on the south. (See article on the Florida Railroad.) The telegraph line to Cuba branches off at this station.

White House—178 miles from Quincy and 11 miles from Jacksonville.

Jacksonville—189 miles from Quincy. Terminus of the J. P. & M. Railroad. Telegraph Office. Boats for all points on the St. Johns River, and connecting with the St. Augustine Railroad at Tocoi, are taken here. (See article on the St. Johns River.)

FROM TALLAHASSEE TO ST. MARKS.

A branch railroad of 21 miles in length, connects Tallahassee with the port of St. Marks, on the Gulf of Mexico.

St. Marks—21 miles from Tallahassee. Telegraph Office. A small settlement. Connection is made here with steamers for New Orleans, Pensacola, Apalachicola, Cedar Keys, Key West and Havana. (See advertisement.)

MIDDLE FLORIDA.

From Fernandina, via Baldwin, to Cedar Keys, by the Atlantic, Gulf and West India Transit Co's Railroad.

The Florida Railroad stretches across the State, from the city of Fernandina in the extreme north-east, to Cedar Keys on the Gulf of Mexico, 154 miles south-west; thus connecting the waters of the Gulf and the Atlantic with an iron link. The road is well built and comfortable, and passes through some of the most picturesque parts of Florida. Through trains leaving daily from either terminus make the passage in twe

The following are the stations on this route:

Fernandina — Telegraph Office. An old but thriving city; situated on the inner or western shore of Amelia Island, and at the mouth of the Amelia River, which divides it from the main land, and forms, with Cumberland Sound, one of the best and safest seaports on the Atlantic coast, south of the Virginia capes. The city was built by the Spaniards. For many years it languished, but the completion of the railroad connection with the Gulf of Mexico gave it a new start, and it is now one of the most promising cities in the South. The population is about 2500. The harbor of Fernandina is so capacious, that, during the war of 1812, when the town was Spanish and neutral, more than three hundred square-rigged vessels were congregated together in its waters at one time. The harbor is land-locked, aud indeed can hold immense fleets in safety from the raging gales of the Atlantic outside. Vessels drawing 19 or 20 feet can cross the bar at high tide, while vessels of the deepest draught can unload at the wharves.

The lumber interest in this city is very considerable and is increasing. There are four large saw mills in operation, and others are contemplated. English capital has lately started a large cotton-ginning establishment, and there is a prospect of the town becoming a large depot for Government naval stores. It is to the market gardener that the neighborhood of Fernandina offers the greatest inducements. Vegetables can be raised, particularly in the winter season, so much earlier than at the North, that they are a very profitable article of shipment to New York.

Fernandina has seven churches, one Episcopal, one Presbyterian, two Methodist, two Baptist and one Roman Catholic. It is the seat of the Episcopal Bishoprick of Florida. A large and flourishing academy for young ladies is under the charge of the Bishop. There is one newspaper published in the city, entitled the *Fernandina Observer*. A good first-class hotel is greatly needed in Fernandina, and any capitalist would find the establishment of such a house abundantly remunerative. At present the rates charged per day are from $2.00 to $3.50, but there are numerous boarding houses where liberal terms can be made by the week or month. The healthfulness of Fernandina cannot be surpassed in the South. The cool sea breeze in summer makes it a delightful residence, while the general mildness of the climate in winter renders it equally attractive.

Direct communication is had with all the principal railroad points in Florida and seaports to the northward; and a new railroad is contemplated from Fernandina to Jacksonville, which will lessen the traveling distance between that place and Savannah. Besides its pleasant climate, Fernandina has, in its neighborhood, some places of historical interest and natural beauty, which make it attractive to visitors. The magnificent sea beach affords at low water a drive of eighteen miles on a road as smooth and hard as the bed of a billiard table. An interesting excursion is to Dungeness, — miles distant; the seat of the illustrious General Nathaniel Greene of Revolutionary memory. The estate was presented to the General by the people of Georgia, in recognition of his services as commander of the Southern provincial army during the most critical period of the struggle. It consists of about 10,000 acres, and has been laid out with great taste and care. The gardens are superb. The visitor can see here how the olive flourishes in the South, making beautiful groves traversed by avenues; also avenues of live oaks, those giants of the forest, hanging with the sombre though graceful Spanish moss, which droops in long festoons from every limb. On the beach, about half a mile from the Dungeness mansion, may be seen the grave of General Henry Lee, of Virginia, the famous " Light Horse Harry " of the Revolution. He died at this place in March, 1818, aged 63 years. A headstone, erected by his son, General Robert E. Lee, the Commander-in-chief of the Confederate armies, marks the spot where the hero is buried.

Hart's Road—12 miles from Fernandina, 142 miles from Cedar Keys. Wood station.

Callahan—27 miles from Fernandina, 127 miles from Cedar Keys. Junction point of the Great Southern R. R. from Jesup to Jacksonville, now under construction. The village has two churches. The station is situated on an extensive marl bed, and is surrounded by a valuable forest of yellow pine, cypress, live oak, white oak, &c. Travelers who have a curiosity to see live rattlesnakes can gratify it in the woods hereabouts.

Baldwin—Telegraph Office. 47 miles from Fernandina, 107 miles from Cedar Keys. The junction with the Jacksonville, Pensacola and Florida Railroad. The City of Jacksonville is only 20 miles distant. Population of this settlement, about 150. It contains two hotels, the Baldwin House and the Florida House, which have accommodations for 100 guests.

Trail Ridge—62 miles from Fernandina, 92 miles from Cedar Keys.

Starke—73 miles from Fernandina, 81 miles from Cedar Keys. Population, 250. There is a church in the village, and three within the distance of a mile, all Methodist. No hotel, but a good boarding house, kept by Mrs. T. B. Hoyt, who charges $1.50 per day or $25 per month. There are a number of lakes from two and a-half to ten miles distant, some of them large with very clear water. Game is scarce, but fresh water fish abound in the lakes. This part of Florida is principally inhabited by small farmers, who cultivate the sea island cotton, corn, sugar cane, sweet oranges, peaches and a variety of garden productions.

Waldo—84 miles from Fernandina and 70 miles from Cedar Keys. Junction of the railroad now being constructed to Tampa Bay. Population, about 125. Has two Baptist and one Methodist churches. No hotel, but board can be obtained in private families, at from $15.00 to $20.00 per month. The village has two mills for ginning cotton. Santa Fe Lake is about two miles distant. It is about nine miles long and four wide, and affords excellent facilities for boating and fishing. About six miles from Waldo there is a natural sink in the land covering about two acres. A stream runs into it continually, and yet there is no visible outlet. The Santa Fe River disappears several miles from the village, and flows under ground, thus forming a natural bridge. The lakes and creeks here about are filled with trout and perch, and the woods with deer, ducks, quails, etc. This neighborhood is remarkable for its healthfulness. The only local disease is the malarial fever, which prevails during the later months of summer, but which is in a mild form and easily controlled by remedies. The climate is peculiarly adapted to sufferers from diseases of the lungs, the air being dry and pleasant.

Gainesville—96 miles from Fernandina, 55 miles from Cedar Keys. Telegraph Office. The largest and most important station on the Florida Railroad, and a favorite resort for invalids. County seat of Alachua County. Population, 1500. The town contains Presbyterian, Baptist, Methodist and Episcopalian churches, three flourishing academies, two newspapers, the *Independent*, republican, and the *New Era*, conservative, and three hotels with good accommodations. The latter are: Oak Hall, Colonel Lemuel Wilson, proprietor; Exchange Hotel, P. Shemwell, proprietor; Beville House, Mrs. S. P. Beville; board, $2.00 to $3.00 per day, or $25.00 to $30.00 per month. There are two livery stables, affording ample means for conveyance into the interior and to the natural curiosities with which the vicinity abounds. The Alachua, a body of water, termed in Florida, a "sink," is the recipient of several streams, with a subterranean passage to the ocean. It is filled with alligators and all kinds of fish, and the surrounding scenery is very charming and romantic. In Alachua County there is a large and beautiful prairie, twenty miles long and five miles wide. The county is the largest in the State, with a population of 20,000. There are twenty-eight public schools. A tri-weekly mail line starts from Gainesville for Tampa on the Gulf. Passengers are taken. There is plenty of game in the woods. Oranges, lemons, limes, grapes, bananas and peaches thrive here. Peach trees sometimes bear at the age of fifteen months, a thing unknown in any other section of the Union. Garden truck is raised in abundance for the Northern markets. Immigrants are welcomed. Land from 75 cents to $50.00 per acre. Newmansville and Micanopy are important towns in the county, which have stage connections with Gainesville.

Archer—113 miles from Fernandina, and 41 miles from Cedar Keys. The Suwanee River is distant about 25 miles. Population, 200. No hotels, but travelers are accommodated at the houses of Joseph S. McDonell and Mrs. Young. There are three Methodist and one Baptist churches. Hereabouts are magnificent pine forests and beautiful prairie views.

Bronson—122 miles from Fernandina, and 32 miles from Cedar Keys. A new place, settled mostly since the war. Population about 100. It is the county seat of Levy County. There is one church (Methodist), and a hotel of limited capacity, the Jackson House, but the fare is excellent. Board can be obtained in private families at about $1.00 per day. Twelve miles from the village is an inexhaustible bed of iron ore, which has not yet been worked. The railroad here passes through some of the finest land in the State, the Gulf hummock, adapted for the culture of sugar cane, cotton, corn, &c. In the neighboring creeks, besides many varieties of fish, there are an abundance of soft-shell turtles, which, when properly prepared, make a very savory and delicious dish.

Otter Creek—135 miles from Fernandina, 19 miles from Cedar Keys.

Palmetto—144 miles from Fernandina, 10 miles from Cedar Keys.

Cedar Keys—154 miles from Fernandina, 126 miles from Jacksonville. The Gulf of Mexico terminus of the

Florida Railroad. Regular packet steamers connect here with New Orleans, Key West and Havana. Population, 400. There are two hotels, the Gulf House, fare $2.50, and the Exchange, $3.00 per day. The Suwanee River enters the Gulf eighteen miles west of Cedar Keys, and the Withlacooche, eighteen miles south. The former is navigable to Ellaville. Cedar Keys is situated on a fine, large bay, which affords excellent facilities for bathing, boating and fishing.

The New Orleans, Florida and Havana Steamship Company dispatch one of the steamers of their line every Saturday morning for Havana, New Orleans and Key West. Passengers desiring to go by these steamers should be in Cedar Keys on Friday night.

THE ST. JOHNS RIVER.

This grand water-course of Eastern Florida, has its source in the springs and swamps of the southern extremity of the peninsula, and flowing northward, for a distance of four hundred miles, turns abruptly eastward in the neighborhood of Jacksonville, and empties into the Atlantic Ocean. Its whole course lies through an extremely level region. For one hundred and fifty miles it has an average width of more than one and a-half miles, and is said to carry a volume of water much larger than does the Rio Grande, which is one thousand miles long. In some places it expands to a width of six miles, nor does it contract at any point to less than a mile, below Lake George.

Many of the tributaries of the St. Johns are navigable to quite a distance by steamboats, and it is believed that this river and its navigable branches give one thousand miles of water transportation. The river scenery is not only beautiful, but to the stranger's eye, has the additional charm of novelty. The luxuriance of the tropical vegetation, the pretty villages nestling amid magnificent shade trees or orange groves along the banks, and the broad, placid waters through which the steamer ploughs its way, combine to make a picture of surpassing loveliness.

The banks of the St. Johns are the principal attraction to the invalids coming to Florida in search of a balmy climate, change of scene and pleasant surroundings. Thousands of visitors from the North are scattered among its towns and villages every winter. The means of access are easy and comfortable. Large steamers ascend as far as Palatka, from which smaller steamers continue the tourist's journey on the St. Johns to Lake Monroe, and on the Oclawaha River to Silver Springs, and the interior lake country.

There are two daily lines from *Jacksonville* to *Palatka* *Hampton* and *Sappho*, leaving t 9.00 A.M. In addition, Brocks & Coxetler's daily line to Enterprise and intermediate landings, leaving at 11.00 A. M., as follows:

Starlight, Mondays and Thursdays; Hattie, Tuesdays and Fridays; D vid Clark, Wednesdays and Saturdays. Steamer Geo. M. Bird, on arrival of A. M. trains, every Wednesday and Saturday from Enterprise and River landings. Steamer Hattie Barker leaves 9.30 A. M. Tuesdays and Fridays, for Melvonville and intermediate landings. Canie leaves Thursdays, for Enterprise and intermediate landings.

Pioneer Line, Steamers Volusia and Daylight. Volusia leaves every Saturday at 11.00 A. M., and Daylight every Tuesday at 11.00 A. M., for Enterprise, Lake Jesup and Lake Harney, connecting there with Hacks, &c. to Indian River. The Lollie Boy, Tuskawilla, Okahumkee and other Steamers are also engaged in transporting passengers and freight to points on the St. John's and Ocklawha Rivers,

JACKSONVILLE, FLA.

General Sketch.—County seat of Duval County, situated 25 miles from the mouth of the St. Johns River on its western bank. The commercial emporium of East Florida, and the largest city on the Atlantic coast of the United States south of Savannah; it is the chief objective point of tourists to the Land of Flowers. The city is regularly incorporated, has a Mayor and Board of Aldermen, and is the seat of the United States District Court and of the Federal Customs and Internal Revenue Offices. Its streets have been regularly laid out, with fine sidewalks and shade trees, and numerous structures, public and private, bespeak its wealth and importance. Within its limits are twelve Churches, three being Baptist, three Methodist, two Episcopalian, two Presbyterian, one Roman Catholic and one Second Advent.

Originally named in honor of General Andrew Jackson, the place remained a small village, though considerably resorted to by invalids for half a century past, until the close of the late war. A census taken by Ex-Senator Osborne, in charge of the Freedmen's Bureau in Florida, in 1866, showed a population of less than 1700, most of them ragged blacks. To-day there is a permanent population of nearly 13,000, and while then there were but five brick buildings in the place there are now to be seen long rows of stores, rivaling those of the Metropolis in the variety of the stocks and the richness of display. No such ratio of growth can be shown by any other city of the Union.

Topography and Suburbs. The rapid growth of Jacksonville has caused it to extend along the bank of the St. Johns River for more than four miles, calling into existence East Jacksonville, Oakland, Wyoming, on the east, and La Villa, Brooklyn and Riverside on the west,

Springfield, a locality in the North of Jacksonville, of more recent growth, is expected to be in time the centre of the growth of fashionable residences of Northern sojourners. The land here slopes from a considerable height southward to Hogan's Creek, the city limit, and commands a fine view of the St. John's River and surrounding country. The villages of Riverside, Reed's Landing, South Shore and Alexandria are reached by ferryboat. Land at either of the points mentioned can be advantageously purchased, and the attention of Northern capitalists has of late years been largely directed to its value as an investment.

Streets—The principal business thoroughfare is Bay Street, and from this, at right angles, branch off the other Streets of Jacksonville. Bay Street, for a distance of three-quarters of a mile, is built up on both sides with solid brick business houses, and is a leading feature of interest to visitors.

Hotels—As might be naturally inferred, a winter resort so generously patronized as Jacksonville, abounds in the best of hotel accommodations and boarding houses, where visitors may find all the comforts and conveniences of life. Prominent among the hotels may be mentioned the St. James (J. R. Campbell, Manager), Grand National Hotel (Geo. McGinly, Proprietor), Carleton House (Stimpson, Devernel & Davis, Proprietors), Windsor Hotel, Metropolitan, Moncrief and St. John's are also commodious and well kept houses.

Educational Establishments—Both the Protestant and Roman Catholic portions of the community are furnished with the means of careful education. For the former St. Mary's Priory, under the personal supervision of the Episcopal Bishop of the Diocese, and for the latter, the St. Joseph's Academy, under the Lady Superior, assisted by the Sisters of the Order of St. Joseph, offer complete courses of study and discipline, without sectarian proselytism, to those whose children's health demand a southern climate.

Commerce and Industries. As a trade centre, this city must, as the outlet for the immense lumber business of the State on the one hand, and its chief port of entry for the merchandise of the world on the other, necessarily retain its pre-eminence, and continually attract to its counters the business of dealers from the interior, who, even now, rarely go as they did once to Savannah or Charleston to buy their goods. Jacksonville merchants show in this, and many other regards, the enterprise which not only deserves but commands success. There are nine large saw mills in operation, for instance, while many others located along the thousand miles of inland navigable water ship their lumber from this port. This fact alone also serves to show the immense inland wealth of this region awaiting development at the hands of enterprise and capital.

Banking facilities are offered at the Banking Houses of D. G. Ambler and Denny & Brown, both on Bay street. There is a Freedman's Saving Bank situated on the corner of Ocean and Bay Streets, and a New National Bank is this year to be started. Among the industrial enterprises may be especially mentioned the manufacture from the palmetto leaf of a fine quality of bank note paper. A shoe factory and a cotton factory are both talked of, and, more important than all, direct steamship communication with New York is seriously contemplated for the coming season,

Nor should mention be forgotten of the novel industry of wild orange champagne manufacture, recently entered upon by Mr. J. H. Paine, a chemist, who has lately made Jacksonville his home. From the refuse of the wine process he also eliminates a valuable wax, and an essential oil which commands a high price.

The Fire Department of Jacksonville is, in its apparatus and *personel*, another unmistakable evidence of the city's enterprise, and includes in its equipage two fine Amoskeag engines and several handsome hose carriages and trucks.

Points of Interest. A visit to Jacksonville would be incomplete without a drive out by the magnificent shell road, cut one hundred feet wide through the pine forest, a distance of four miles, to the now famous Moncrief's Springs, the waters of which possess rare medicinal virtues, especially beneficial for sufferers by malarial complaints. The place is said to have derived its name from a French Jew who, having married an Indian maiden, was here robbed and slain by her relatives. Recently a company was formed, with the Mayor of Jacksonville at its head, for the purpose of improving the grounds about the springs, and rendering them a pleasant resort for Jacksonville visitors. Two fine baths, or pools, have been established with dressing rooms attached; a restaurant, pavilion and orchestra stand have been erected, and now there are few, if any, pleasanter springs than Moncrief's to be found anywhere throughout the South.

Visitors desiring to carry home mementoes of Jacksonville, will find at the gallery of Messrs. Wood & Bickle, on Bay street, a fine assortment of stereoscopic views of the many interesting points in and about the city.

At D n Greenleaf's Museum of Florida Curiosities, also on Bay street, they may pass, too, an instructive and entertaining visit in inspecting his valuable collection of living reptiles, birds and wild animals. This museum, where crowds daily assemble, is among the fashionable resorts of the city during the winter season.

Daily Line Between Jacksonville and Palatka.
—The Old Dominion Steamship Company's New and Elegant Saloon Steamer HAMPTON, Capt. A. W. Starke, Purser, James M. Gallagher, will leave Clark's Wharf, Jacksonville, daily, 9.00 A. M. (Sundays excepted) for Palatka, touching both ways at Green Cove Springs and Tocoi, connecting at the latter place with trains to and from St. Augustine, and at Palatka with the U. S. Mail Steamer "Pastime," tri weekly, for Entetprise and intermediate landings on the upper St. John's.

JOHN CLARK, Agent, Jacksonville, Fla

THE ST. JOHNS RIVER—CONTINUED.

Mulberry Grove—The first landing-place after leaving Jacksonville, 12 miles distant, on the west bank. A beautiful grove.

Mandarin—15 miles from Jacksonville, on the east bank, a village of 200 inhabitants, one of the oldest settlements on the river; has several stores and two or three fine orange groves. This place is of interest to Northern visitors as being the winter residence of Mrs. Harriet Beecher Stowe. Her house is near the bank, a few rods to the left of the shore end of the pier. It is a moderate-sized cottage of dark brown color. A Catholic Convent has recently been established at this point by the Bishop of Florida, and is now inhabited by the Sisters.

Hibernia—25 miles from Jacksonville, on the west bank. This is quite a resort for invalids. Mrs. Fleming has a large, commodious house, which will accommodate about forty boarders and is one of the first to fill up.

Magnolia—28 miles from Jacksonville, on the west bank; a beautiful place, with a fine hotel kept by Mr. Houghton. With the contiguous cottages about eighty guests can be accommodated. Near by is Magnolia Point, one of the highest points of land extending into the river between Jacksonville and Palatka. A short distance north of Magnolia Point a navigable stream, called Black Creek, empties into the St. Johns. Small steamers from Jacksonville make weekly trips up Black Creek as far as Middleburg. Large quantities of lumber are floated down this stream to a market. The banks abound with alligators.

Green Cove Springs—30 miles from Jacksonville, on the west bank; one of the most popular resorts on the river. The Union House will accommodate comfortably about fifty guests. There are other hotels and several good boarding houses. Rates at the hotels, $3.00 per day; at the boarding houses, per week, $10 to $15. One of the attractions at this place is the Spring, which is held in high esteem for its health-giving qualities. The water has a temperature of about 75 degrees; is as clear as crystal and has a slight sulphurous taste, not unpleasant. Facilities are afforded to both sexes for bathing at the Spring. Green Cove promises to become in time a flourishing and populous village.

Hogarth's Wharf—35 miles from Jacksonville, on the east bank; a post-office and wood landing.

Picolata—45 miles from Jacksonville, on the east bank. This small settlement is the site of an ancient Spanish city, of which scarce one vestige remains. Two centuries ago, it was the main depot of supply for the Spanish plantations of the up country, and through it, were shipped to St. Augustine and abroad, such products as the settlers raised. The Franciscan monks erected a splendid church here and some religious houses for their order. Opposite Picolata, on the western bank, are the remains of a great earthwork fort belonging to the Spanish era.

Tocoi—53 miles from Jacksonville, on the east bank. The depot of the St. Augustine Railroad. The distance to St. Augustine is 15 miles, and trains connecting with the river boats run through in 40 minutes. Before the use of locomotives the time required to make this journey was two hours. There are a few objects of interest to be seen in the time allowed here, and the restaurant of Mr. Thomas can be recommended to tourists.

Palatka—75 miles from Jacksonville, west bank. Population 1000 (Telegraph office). It is the largest town on the St. Johns above Jacksonville, and is the head of navigation for ocean steamers, which here transfer their freight and passengers for the upper St. Johns and Ocklawaha rivers. It occupies an elevated site, and extends about half a mile along the bank. The town has numerous stores doing a good business, two hotels, the St. Johns, (a first-class house, conducted by P. & H. Petermann,) and the Putnam House, a weekly paper, the *Eastern Herald*, a ship yard, and several mills and other industries. The business houses are large and attractive in appearance, and the wharves, which are numerous, are lined with commodious warehouses, in which is constantly stored merchandise from most of the Atlantic seaports. Palatka is an important commercial point, and is each year becoming more so.

Steamers run from Palatka to Dunn's Lake, and also up the Ocklawaha River to Silver Springs, Ocala, and the head of navigation, a distance of 180 miles. Opposite to Palatka, a distance of a mile and a half, and accessible by boat at all times, is Col. Hart's famous Orange Grove of six acres, said to be the most highly cultivated of any in the South. In different parts of the grove can be seen every variety of tropical fruit, including a fine grove of bananas. From a single orange tree Col. Hart gathered last year 4500 oranges. No visitor staying over a day at Palatka should fail to visit this beautiful spot.

Welaka—100 miles from Jacksonville and 20 miles from Palatka, on the east bank, is the site first, of an old Indian village, and afterwards, of a flourishing Spanish settlement. It is near the entrance to Dunn's Lake, and also to the Ocklawaha River. The scenery along the Ocklawaha is very wild and picturesque, and is much admired by tourists. There are some magnificent plantations on the banks, and large quantities of cotton and sugar are raised. Silver Spring is a basin of beautiful, clear and deep water. This the site of a Seminole village of 600 inhabitants.

Lake George—After leaving Welaka, the river widens into Little Lake George, four miles wide and seven miles long, and then into Big Lake George, one of the loveliest sheets of water in the world; twelve miles wide and eighteen miles long. It is dotted with pretty islands, one of them called Rembert, being seventeen hundred acres in extent, and having one of the largest orange groves on the river. The banks of Lake George are musical with the song and brilliant with the plumage of the Southern birds. Flocks of herons, the white curlew, the crane, the pelican, the loon and the paroquet may be seen. The latter can be bought of the negroes.

Volusia—5½ miles from Lake George, and 65 miles from Palatka, on the east bank; a wood station, with a considerable settlement back from the river. This is the site of another ancient Spanish city, wiped out by the wars of the past, so that not a trace remains. It was the principal point on the line of travel between St. Augustine and the Musquito Inlet country. The modern village was settled in 1818. During the Seminole war a fort was built here, and from this post General Eustis, in command of the left wing of the army, composed mostly of regulars and drafted three months' men from South Carolina and Georgia, set out to cross the country to the Withlacoochee, to join General Scott. After a brief and fruitless campaign of three months, General Scott and his army recrossed the river at Volusia on their way to St. Augustine.

Means can be had at Volusia to get to New Smyrna and Indian River on the coast; a famous country for the hunter. New Smyrna is celebrated as the spot settled by Dr. Turnbull and his colony of 1500 Minorcans, in the year 1767. Turnbull's wife being a native of Smyrna, in Asia, the settlement was named New Smyrna. The crop cultivated by Turnbull was indigo, of which he raised thousands of dollars' worth annually. These colonists not being dealt with according to contract, all abandoned the settlement and located in and near St. Augustine, where their descendants now reside. The only permanent monument left by Turnbull is a large canal, draining the swamp that bears his name into the Hillsboro' River at New Smyrna.

Orange Grove—10 miles from Lake George. Wood landing.

Hawkinsville—20 miles from Lake George. Wood landing.

Blue Spring—33 miles from Lake George. Wood landing. Near here is one of the largest springs in the State. The water boils up from a bottom eighty feet wide, and forms a considerable river. The spring is several hundred yards from the St. Johns, but the stream flowing from the spring is large enough, at its confluence at the river, for the steamers to float in it. It is a most interesting sight to look over the side of the steamer, into the crystal-clear water, and observe the every-day life of the shoals of fish below, as they flit here and there, seeking a living, making love to and war on each other, quite unconscious of the lookers-on in the element over their heads.

Mellonville—125 miles from Palatka, and 200 miles from Jacksonville, on the west bank of Lake Monroe. One of the most important landings on the Upper St. Johns. It was formerly the site of Fort Mellon, built during the Indian War. There are two hotels here. The orange groves in the neighborhood are handsome and productive, and have induced the establishment at this point of a manufactory of a new and health-giving beverage known as "Orange Bitters," and which as a tonic for invalids are pronounced by physicians as unsurpassed. The advertisement of the proprietor, Mr. J. J. Hite, will be found elsewhere. Lake Monroe, upon which Mellonville is situated, is twelve miles long and five miles wide. It is crowded with fish of many varieties, and the opportunities for rare sport to the angler, are unsurpassed. Wild fowls are likewise abundant.

Enterprise—Almost directly opposite Mellonville, on the east bank of Lake Monroe; is 130 miles from Palatka and 205 miles from Jacksonville, and the head of regular steamboat navigation. Here is one of the best and most popular hotels on the river, the Brock House; a large comfortable building, capable of entertaining one hundred guests. It is usually crowded during the winter. Attached to it are a billiard saloon and a ten-pin alley. The rates for board rank from $15.00 to $20 00 per week. according to rooms. The Green Spring, at Old Enterprise, about a mile from the Brock House, is worth a visit, as well as the orange groves in the vicinity. The Spring is of a delicate green color, and at times transparent. It is nearly eighty feet in diameter, and fully one hundred feet deep. The waters are sulphurous, and few fish live in them. Enterprise is the great headquarters for the sportsman. Fishing and hunting expeditions are fitted out here for the upper lakes and the Indian River country. Horses and boats are kept on hire, and during the winter a small steamboat makes frequent excursions to Lakes Jessup and Harney, taking parties who wish to enjoy the ravishing scenery and indulge in that novel and exciting sport, alligator shooting. The run up to Lake Harney and back, can be made in a day. Lake Jessup, which is in the neighborhood of Lake Harney, is seventeen miles long by five miles wide, and is so shallow, that it cannot be entered by a boat drawing over three feet of water. The St. John's River has its rise in the Everglades, fully 120 miles further south than Enterprise, but tourists do not usually ascend beyond Lake Harney, twelve miles from Enterprise. The climate in this locality is perceptibly milder than below. The winter resembles very much the months of May and June at the North, though without their occasional scorching heat.

The Southern Inland Navigation and Improvement Company have contracted to deepen the waters of the St. Johns, from Enterprise, as far as Lake Washington. This much-needed improvement will give inland communication with Indian River, Sand Point, Mosquito Inlet, Indian River Inlet, Susannah, Jupiter Inlet, and the capes, and opens up the entire south-east coast of Florida to the extremity of the Peninsula. To the tourist in search of adventure, this section of the State presents a magnificent field. The Indian River is alive with every variety of fish that inhabit the Southern waters, and the woods abound in game.

ST. AUGUSTINE.

Since the completion of the railroad from St. Augustine to Tocoi, on the St. Johns River, access to this picturesque and beautiful old Spanish town has been easy, pleasant and rapid. The regular packet steamers up the St. Johns River leave Jacksonville at nine o'clock daily, Sundays excepted; and connect at Tocoi (57 miles from Jacksonville) with the St. Augustine Railroad. The train runs through from Tocoi to St. Augustine in forty minutes. The distance between Tocoi and St. Augustine is fifteen miles. Through fare from Jacksonville, *via* steamer and railroad, $3.00. Meals and staterooms $1.00 extra.

St. Augustine, the most ancient town in North America, is situated on a peninsula nearly surrounded by the St. Sebastian River and St. Augustine Bay. The population is 2,000 souls, mostly of Spanish and Minorcan descent. Across the Bay is Anastasia Island. The town was founded by Menendez, the Spanish Governor of Florida, in 1565, which was forty-three years before the settlement of Jamestown, in Virginia, and fifty-five years before the landing of the Pilgrims on Plymouth Rock. St. Augustine has had an eventful history. First, it was laid waste by the French, under De Gourgues; in 1580, it was attacked and plundered by the English, under Sir Francis

Drake. In 1611, it was pillaged by the Indians. In 1665, the English buccaneer, Davis, sacked it, after the inhabitants had taken refuge in the fort. In 1702, Governor Moore, of the English Colony of South Carolina, invaded Florida, and attacked the city, but was baffled by the fort. In 1712, the inhabitants suffered from a famine in consequence of the non-arrival of supply ships from Spain. In 1725, the Georgians, under Colonel Palmer, were beaten off.) In 1740, General Oglethorpe, the Governor of Georgia, laid regular siege to the place, planting his batteries on Anastasia Island and bombarding the fort for thirty-eight days. He failed to force the Spaniards to surrender, and retired. The city passed into British possession, by treaty, in 1763, and held a British garrison during our Revolutionary war. In 1784, it was re-ceded to Spain, and in 1819 transferred to the United States. During the late war between the States, it changed masters three times.

Hotels—St. Augustine, like Jacksonville, is provided with the very best of hotel accommodations, affording the Northern visitor all the comforts and luxuries which modern civilization can furnish. The St. Augustine Hotel (E. E. Vaill, Proprietor), fronting upon the bay and overlooking the ocean, seats 300 guests, and has been entirely refitted and refurnished thoughout. The Magnolia House (W. W. Palmer, Proprietor,) is also a first-class establishment, deservedly popular with winter tourists to St. Augustine.

Old Town Wall—Built by the Spaniards two centuries ago. It protected the town on its northern side, and extended across the peninsula from shore to shore. The gateway of the old wall still stands, and is a picturesque and imposing ruin, with ornamented lofty towers and loop-holed sentry-boxes. The ditch is clearly marked.

Fort Marion—The old Spanish fort once called San Juan. It was begun in 1620, and built principally by the forced labor of Indian slaves who toiled on it for one hundred years. It stands on the sea front, at the upper

Interior of Fort Marion.

end of the town, and its material is almost wholly the Coquina rock, quarried on Anastasia Island. A ramble through its heavy casements, its crumbling Roman chapel, with elaborate portico and inner altar and holy-water niches, its dark passages, gloomy vaults, and more recently-discovered dungeons, bring you ready credence of its many traditions of inquisitorial tortures. In one of the arched dungeons, discovered by accident, beneath the walls of the fort, was found a sealed up stone doorway, which being dug away, gave access to an inner dungeon. In this place were found two cages, in each of which were skeletons, one of them that of a female. One of these is now preserved in the Smithsonian Institute, the other was interred on the north side of the fort. A visit to the fort by moonlight also is recommended.

Cathedral.—The old Catholic cathedral, with its quaint Moorish belfry, its chime of four bells in separate niches, and its clock, together forming a cross, and its antique interior, is one of the most interesting objects in St. Augustine. The oldest of the bells is marked 1682.

Other Churches.—The Episcopalians have a neat chapel on the Plaza. There are also Methodist, Baptist and Presbyterian churches in the city.

The Plaza.—A fine public square in the centre of the city is called the "Plaza de la Constitution. On it stand the ancient markets, and it is faced by the cathedral, the old palace, the convent, and the Episcopal church. In the middle is a monument erected in honor of the Spanish Liberal Constitution. Effigies of John Hancock and Samuel Adams were burned on this spot by the British troops early in the Revolution. The Plaza is a very pleasant resort for idlers, who will find a firm, green turf for lounging, benches and shade trees. The visit by moonlight is enchanting.

The Palace, or old Government house of the Spanish era, on the Plaza, is now used as the post-office, Court, St. Aug. Library and Reading Rooms, and Peabody School.

Barracks—occupied by United States troops, said to have once been a monastery or convent.

Convents.—There are three, the old Spanish convent of St. Mary's, the one in the rear of the palace, a tasteful edifice built of Coquina, and largest of all, the new convent on St. George street, near the Barracks.

Cemeteries.—The old Huguenot burying-ground is a place of much interest. In the military burying-ground, under three pyramids of Coquina, stuccoed and whitened, are the ashes of Major Dade and 107 men of his command, who were massacred by Osceola and his band.

Sea-Wall.—A fine sea-wall of nearly a mile in length, built of Coquina, with a coping of granite, protects the entire bay front of the city, and affords a delightful promenade on a moonlight evening. In full view of this is the old light-house on Anastasia Island, built more than a century ago, and now surmounted by a fine revolving lantern. A new light-house, 160 feet high, has also been erected here by the Government.

The Bay and Anastasia Island.—Boating on the bay is a favorite amusement on moonlight nights. The sail by day across the bay to Anastasia Island is charming. Beautiful shells of all descriptions may be gathered on the beach, and sea-mosses and lichens may be collected for albums.

Streets.—They are nearly all quite narrow; one, which is nearly a mile long, being but fifteen feet wide. Many of the houses, with high roof and dormer windows, have hanging balconies along their second stories, which seem almost to touch each other across the narrow street.

Improvements.—Half a million dollars have been expended on improvements, public and private, in St. Augustine since 1870. Charlotte, St. George and Bay streets are all interesting thoroughfares. Among the private residences recently completed may be named those of Henry Ball, of Ball, Black & Co., costing $50,000; of John Howard, costing $30,000; and of Wm. H. Aspinwall, costing $25,000. Speculation in land has been rife for some time, and the natural charms, added to its historic, will probably make St. Augustine soon outstrip in development the younger cities of the State.

WESTERN FLORIDA.

The country west of the Apalachicola River has not yet been brought into railroad communication with the other parts of the State. Its comparative isolation was the cause of the recent movement in favor of annexing it to Alabama. The extension of lines of the Jacksonville, Pensacola and the Mobile Railroad, will soon remove any feeling of discontent which may exist in Western Florida.

Apalachicola.—This city was formerly the seat of a very considerable trade. It was the shipping port for that rich cotton-growing region lying on the Chattahoochie and Flint Rivers, which empty into the Apalachicola River, and thus into Apalachicola Bay. The Chattahoochee is navigable as far up as Columbus, Georgia; a distance of 367 miles. The building of numerous railroads in lower Georgia and Alabama, which tapped the river line, diverted trade from this old city to Mobile and Savannah. The population has decreased, but it still can boast about 1000 inhabitants. Owing to its fine site there is no reason why, with capital and energy, its former prosperity should not be revived.

Marianna.—County seat of Jackson County. This town is situated on the Chipola River, an affluent of the Apalachicola, and navigable at certain seasons by small craft to Marianna. The business of this town is ordinarily done through Bellevue and Neal's Landing, about 18 miles distant, on the Chattahoochee.

The extension of the Jacksonville, Pensacola and Mobile Railroad will pass through Marianna, and must very much increase its prosperity, already ensured by the fertility of the adjacent country.

Pensacola—The principal city of Western Florida. Population, 2,000. It is situated on Pensacola Bay, and is enjoying a lucrative and growing trade. At the entrance of the bay lies Santa Rosa Island, upon which is built Fort Pickens, the scene of one of the most famous sieges of the earlier years of the late war between the States. The city was laid out by the English in 1763. Pensacola may be reached from Jacksonville and Eastern Florida by means of the railroad to St. Marks on the Gulf, and regular packet steamer from St. Marks to Pensacola Bay. The Pensacola and Louisville Railroad connects at Pollard with the Mobile and Montgomery Railroad.

The following observations upon the future of Pensacola are taken from a pamphlet issued by the "New City Company:"

"The City of Pensacola has natural advantages which destine it to become, by rapid strides, the *Chicago of the South*. It is situated on the north coast of the Gulf of Mexico, in latitude 30 deg. 28 m. north, and longitude 87 deg. 22 m. west of Greenwich, only ten miles from the open sea. Its thoroughly land-locked harbor covers an area of over two hundred square miles, being about thirty miles long, and from five to eight miles in width, having unsurpassed anchorage, and a depth of from thirty to thirty-five feet. The entrance to the harbor is about half a mile wide, with an average depth on the bar of *twenty-four feet*. The same depth is readily secured at the wharfage line of the city. A laden ship of largest tonnage can approach the city at any time in the year, or leaving its wharves can be in the open sea in an hour-and-a-half.

"The rapid development of the iron mines of Alabama, whose natural outlet to the markets of the world is the port of Pensacola, will not only contribute a considerable quota to the commerce of this port, but will, in connection with the Florida forests, furnish superior material for ship-building, which, at no distant day, must rival in extent the similar industry of northern ports; the proximity and cheapness of all material required giving builders in this locality peculiar advantages."

Southern Florida.

Southern or Tropical Florida is, properly speaking, that part of the State lying south of latitude 28 deg. north. It comprises an area of 20,000 square miles, and has a population of about 9,000 inhabitants. About half of this population reside on the Island of Key West and the neighboring Keys and islands extending into the Gulf of Mexico, and are engaged in the business of wrecking and fishing. The raising of cattle upon the main-land is the all-absorbing business of the inhabitants, who reside from 30 to 40 miles apart, and allow the cattle to graze on the public domain. The herds are immense; in Manatee County alone, there are 100,000 head of cattle.

The main-land is level and divided into hummocks, pine openings and prairies. The hummocks are very rich, and are covered over with a dense growth of timber; consisting of live oak, water oaks, magnolia, bay, etc. The soil is sandy. The pine openings are covered with scattering pines and a grass which affords fine pasturage. The prairie lands occupy the interior portion of the State, bordering upon the Kissimee River, the head waters of the St. Johns, and the upper Caloosahatchee. They are dotted over with small clumps of hummocks, containing from one to five acres each, which give beauty and variety to the scenery, and afford shelter during the heat of the day to innumerable herds of deer and cattle. There are also numerous small lakes of pure water, filled with fish, some of which are only a few rods in extent, while others are from two to ten miles in length. These prairies are the paradise of the herdsmen and the hunters.

This section of Florida is capable of producing all the different products of the West Indies. There is a constant sea-breeze off the Gulf Stream, commencing about eight o'clock, A. M., and lasting until nearly sundown. The climate is very exhilarating. The thermometer averages, the year round, 73 deg. and the extremes are 57 deg. and 92 deg.

A railroad is projected from Jacksonville, along the St. John's River into Southern Florida. At present, the means of getting to the harbors, on the extreme southern coast, are by sailing vessels from Jacksonville, Key West and New Orleans, or overland, by the mail carrier's conveyances from Gainesville on the Florida Railroad, and Enterprise on the Upper St. John's River.

The following are some of the most notable places in Southern Florida:—

Tampa Bay—On the western coast, is a noble harbor for the largest vessels, and is about 40 miles long. Towards the interior it divides into two branches, called Little Tampa and Hillsborough Bay. It is dotted with small islands, the pleasantest of which is Egmont. In the waters of Tampa Bay enormous quantities of fish and turtles may be found. In shoal places the fish are so numerous that they impede the passage of boats. Sea fowl are exceedingly numerous; the beautiful flamingoes, in particular, appear in long files drawn up on the beach, like bands of soldiers in red uniforms. The village of Tampa has regular mail communication with Gainesville, and passengers avail themselves of the mail wagon for transit. A railroad is projected to Waldo, on the Cedar Keys and Fernandina Railroad; when it is completed, Tampa will become one of the most important ports on the Gulf.

Charlotte Harbor, or Boca Grande, on the western coast, south of Tampa Bay. It is about 25 miles long, and eight to ten miles wide, and is sheltered from the sea by several islands. The entrance between Boca Grande Key and Gasperillo is six fathoms deep and three-quarters of a mile wide.

The fisheries in and around Charlotte Harbor are very valuable, and may be made more so. Probably a thousand persons could find profitable employment. The fish are caught with seines. The finest oysters on the coast are gathered here.

Alpativkee Swamp, upon the head waters of the St. Lucie River, is the only swamp of any magnitude in Tropical Florida.

Indian River is a vast lagoon along the Atlantic coast of Florida, extending a distance of nearly 100 miles. In some places it is four miles wide, and in others, not more than fifty yards wide. The Indian River country is filled with game, and is a celebrated resort of the sportsman.

Lake Okee-cho-bee—A large, wild, solitary lake, near the everglades. Its length is twenty miles.

The Everglades—Situated almost in the southern extremity of the peninsula, is a vast shallow lake, overgrown with grass, pond lilies and other aquatic plants, interspersed with innumerable small islands, of from one to one hundred acres each. These islands are principally hummock lands, covered over with a growth of live and water-oaks and cocoa plums, with an undergrowth of morning-glories, grapes and other vines, and are extremely fertile. The water is from four inches to four feet deep, and is very clear and pure. In many places are channels and sinks where the water is from ten to fifty feet deep; these holes are well supplied with fish, of which the trout is the most desirable. Alligators and turtle are abundant, and panthers, wild-cats, and bears are quite numerous.

Flowers of the sweetest fragance, and of every hue and color, greet the eye. The border and outer margin of the Everglades is prairie, of from one-fourth to one mile in breadth, and comprises some of the finest and richest land in America, having once been a portion of the Everglades, and formed by the receding of the waters. During the Indian war the Everglades were the last retreat of the Seminoles, and it was with the utmost difficulty that the government dislodged them, so well adapted were the almost hidden islands for defence and concealment.

Biscayne Bay—At the end of the peninsula, and emptying into Barnes' Sound and Florida Bay, is an excellent harbor for all vessels drawing less than ten feet of water. It can be entered at all times. Great quantities of turtle and sponges of the finest variety are secured here. The sponges and turtle taken from these waters are valued at $100,000 per annum. Lieutenant Governor Gleason says of the Biscayne Bay country: "The pure water, the chalybeate and other mineral springs, the magnificent beauty of its scenery, the salubrity and equability of its climate, must make Biscayne Bay, at no distant day, the resort of the invalid, the tourist, and the lover of adventure."

The Keys.—These are a series of islands, extending along the south coast, from Cape Florida to the Dry Tortugas, lying between the main-land and the Florida Reefs, and within three to five miles of the Gulf Stream. They are of uniform character, being of coral formation and very rocky. Some are only a few acres in extent, while others contain as many as 15,000 acres. Cayo Largo is the largest. These Keys are only a few feet above tide-water, and are mostly covered with a growth of hardwood timber. The land is too rocky to admit of general cultivation.

Key West—(The city and port of.) Telegraph Office. Is situated on the island of the same name, which is seven miles long and one-and-a-half wide. It is eleven feet above the sea level. The population of the city is about 3,000 It has a large trade in sponges, turtles and fruits, and is a place of some manufacturing importance. There are twelve or fifteen cigar factories, making in the aggregate thirty to thirty-five thousand of the best Havana cigars per diem. There is also a manufactory in successful operation, for canning the pineapple—the only one in the United States. From five to eight thousand cans are put up daily. Key West has five churches and the usual public buildings. The United States Admiralty Court sits here. Two newspapers are published, the *Dispatch*, democratic, and the *Guardian*, republican. There are a few lakes on the island, and several beautiful drives. The land is covered in mid-winter with the greenest of foliage, and tropical flowers grow in profusion. The climate hereabouts is mild and agreeable, the thermometer ranging from 79 to 86 degrees in summer, and 48 to 60 degrees in winter. The island is much visited by invalids. Constant communication is had with New York, New Orleans, Havana, Galveston and Cedar Keys by packet steamers. The passage to Havana occupies but a few hours. The New Orleans, Cedar Keys and Havana steamers afford weekly connection with all points in Upper and Middle Florida, by means of the Florida Railroad. The principal hotels in Key West are the Russell House and the Leland Hotel, recently erected by a stock company. Board can be obtained in numerous private families at reasonable rates.

The Dry Tortugas islands, at the extreme end of the Florida Keys, and extending some distance into the Gulf of Mexico. They were used as a penal place for Confederate prisoners during the late war, and several of the Lincoln conspirators were confined there. They are forlorn, barren rocks, defended by fortifications, and ornamented (?) with a light house.

St, John's River by Daylight.

The **OLD DOMINION** Steamship Company's New and Elegant Saloon Steamer,

HAMPTON,

Leaves **Clark's Wharf**, Jacksonville, at 9:00 A. M. daily, (except Sunday), for

PALATKA AND RETURN.
TOUCHING BOTH WAYS AT
Green Cove Springs and Tocoi,

Connecting at Tocoi with Trains to and from St. Augustine. Connection made on Monday, Wednesday, and Friday with U. S. Mail Steamer

PASTIME,

Leaving Palatka on Tuesday, Thursday and Saturday mornings for Enterprise and intermediate Landings off the Upper St. Johns —Thus making the entire trip on the river by daylight.

Through Tickets at Usual Rates (including meals on steamers and Hotel Coupons—acceptable for the night's Board and lodging at any hotel in Palatka), sold on board.

Also connecting with steamer EUPHEMIA, at Palatka, every day (Sunday excepted) for Crescent City and the Halifax River.

JOHN CLARK, Agent.

A. J. HEIDRICK, Agent, Palatka.
W. H. STANFORD, Secretary.
    Greenwich and Fulton, Streets, New York.

From Bachelder's Popular Resorts and How to Reach Them. (Ill.)

FORTRESS MONROE, HAMPTON ROADS AND VICINITY.

"Fortress Monroe and its immediate surroundings, to Americans certainly, and to a large number of Europeans, have now become classic. It was here the Army of the Potomac first landed in Virginia on its memorable march up the Peninsula, undergoing all the trials and sufferings of a protracted and bloody war. It was here that four years later this same army embarked for the homes they so longed to reach, with peace again ruling o'er the nation. Here, too, under the eyes of thousands of anxious watchers, the great battle of the 'Merrimac' and 'Monitor' was fought. Many residents at 'Old Point Comfort' give vivid descriptions of every event in that mighty conflict, and mark the steps of its progress to the listener with vivid scenes of it before him. The Fortress itself, the largest in the United States, is a grand feature in the attractiveness of the locality and contains within it many objects of the greatest interest to the visitor. Its extensive and beautiful parade ground, shaded with live-oaks; its slopes are coated with green from March until November, and its garrison makes it very popular. The famed Artillery School with the music of an excellent band at morning guard mount and the evening dress parade, give to the visitor pleasure to be found at very few resorts in the country. There is within the fortress, also, a Museum containing objects of great interest to the civilian as well as to the soldier, and many hours may be pleasantly and profitably passed by the visitor in looking over the collection. The drives in the vicinity to the Hampton Normal School, the National Military Home, the National Cemetery and to and through the town of Hampton, are over good roads, and also command many exceedingly interesting landscape views. In the town of Hampton is one of the oldest churches in our country. The incriptions on some of its tombs in its cemetery bearing date as early as 1658.

For the invalid, as well as the robust pleasure seeker, the climate at Old Point Comfort is unsurpassed for salubrity. The invalid en route for the warmer climate of Florida to recuperate, or returning therefrom, and fearing to face the rigors of an uncertain month in spring at the North, may find a resting place at Fortress Monroe free from all dangers of sudden and violent change in temperature. Boating and fishing may be enjoyed on and in the broad waters of Hampton roads and Chesapeake bay, and the fish are very plentiful and excellent in character. The Hampton Bar and Lynnhaven oysters, deservedly celebrated wherever this luxury is known, are here found in abundance. The bathing is also very fine, the beach being of an easy and continuous slope and unusually free from large pebbles.

"The Hygeia Hotel, lately built and this year enlarged and having ample accomodations for five hundred guests, at Fortress Monroe, or Old Point Comfort as it was generally named by visitors in *ante-bellum* times, takes the place of the one of that name which was in existence before the war, and was patronized by many of our people from all sections of the Union. This hotel is most thoroughly built and elegantly furnished, and its situation is admirable, far superior to the old Hygeia, and is in all its appointments every way worthy of its beautiful locality. It stands upon the beach at the head of the broad and substantial landing provided by the National Government for the various steamers which stop here from fifteen to twenty time daily to land their passengers and mails. From its balconies and corridors which have a water frontage of over eighteen hundred feet, the view of Hampton roads and Chesapeake bay is unsurpassed; even Cape Henry and Cape Charles lighthouses may be seen on a clear day, or their lights by night, without the aid of a glass. Vessels of all classes, steam and sail, American and foreign, are passing at all times or riding at their anchors in sight faom every room. The ever changing scenes from the balconies are a source of never ending interest and pleasure. In conducting the hotel every effort is made by the proprietor to insure the comfort and pleasure of his guests, and to make the 'Hygeia' in every respecworthy of patronage. The table is supplied in abuntdance with every delicacy of a locality rich with edibles rare in more northern latitudes, and facilities are provided for bathing, boating and fishing, all of which can be reached literally at the doorsteps of the hotel."

Aiken, S. C.

AIKEN is a thriving village of 2,000 inhabitants, situated on the South Carolina Railroad, 120 miles north-west of Charleston, and 17 miles south-east of Augusta.

It was incorporated before the war, and is governed by an Intendant and six wardens. Occupying one of the most commanding positions in the State, being 600 feet above tide water, and 400 feet above (the Savannah River at) Augusta, it has been aptly called the "Village of Hills."

Immense forests of pine surround it on all sides, and these yield an aroma, which, with the dry invigorating air and equable climate, have rendered Aiken a very favorably known winter resort for invalids.

The main thoroughfare, called Park Avenue, extends, with an even width of 200 feet, for over one mile, and from this at right angles branch the streets, all laid out with a width of 150 feet.

At the extreme western end of Park Avenue, seated on the very brow of a hill commanding an extensive prospect, is the HIGHLAND PARK HOTEL, kept by Mr. B. P. CHATFIELD, (also proprietor of the PLANTERS HOTEL, at Augusta, Ga.)

The house has recently been enlarged and supplied with new furniture, the bed-room sets being of black walnut, having spring bed and hair mattress. Pure spring water conducted to all parts of the building, and drainage from the premises is perfect, the greatest care having been taken in perfecting this important department. Bed-rooms and Parlors arranged in suits are desirable as to location and size, there being none but outside rooms, all having open fireplaces and sunny exposure, Saloon Parlor arranged for private theatricals; Gas and Electrical Bells in every room; Bath-room on each floor. Five stairways leading to upper stories offer sufficient egress. Billiard-Room, Bowling-Alley, Croquet-Grounds, and a well stocked Livery-Stable connected with the Hotel. The table is abundantly supplied and the cooking department carefully attended to.

Exposed as it is to the South, the sun, in a clear day, seems to shine with a special brilliancy on its broad piazzas, which, with the corridors and halls, exceed a quarter of a mile in length.

To the invalid in search of health, Aiken offers the most favorable inducements, and is not without attractions to those who visit the Sunny South for relaxation from business or avoidence of Northern Winter.

Apart from the HIGHLAND PARK HOTEL, there are ample accommodations for visitors. Immediately opposite the Railroad Depot stands the Carleton Hotel, favorably known to visitors, and excellent and well appointed boarding houses are scattered throughout the village. Fronting both sides of Main street are numerous stores, well stocked with all necessary articles, as well as those of luxury, and among them are two pharmaceutical establishments, fitted up in a style that might well become those of a large city, whose proprietors are always ready to fill any prescription ordered by the skilful physicians residing in the place.

The modest, neat little churches, of which there are seven, are indeed ornamental to the "Village of the Hills," and comprise an Episcopal, Presbyterian, Methodist, Baptist, Roman Catholic, and two plain edifices for colored denominations. A Lyceum, capable of seating four hundred persons, through its private theatrical entertainments, contributes materially to the pleasure and gatification of the residents of Aiken, and those who have selected the hill country of Carolina as their Winter home. Four livery stables afford an ample supply of horses and vehicles for riding and driving over the numberless roads which radiate in every direction from the village. A large grove in which are erected buildings for the convenience and enjoyment of the Aiken Schuetzen Club, is but a few minutes walk from the Hotel. For daily Railroad trains between Charleston and Augusta, to which may be added a special accommodation for Augusta, which leaves Aiken at 9:10 A. M., returning at 3:30 P. M.

With attributes thus enumerated, it must be obvious to every traveler that Aiken is tuthfully entitled to the warm encomiums that have been awarded it; that its rapid growth within the past few years has been. a healthy one; and that it offers more than ordinary inducements to those who seek in the balmy climate of the South a contrast to the cold and unpleasant Winters of the North.

WILMINGTON, N. C.

This beautiful city, situated on the Cape Fear River [30 miles from its mouth] is the largest city in the State, and its commercial advantages are second to none on the southern coast. Large fleets of sailing vessels of all nationalities are constantly arriving and departing from this port. It is the largest naval store depot in the world. The climate is delightful, rivaling even Florida. The thermometers seldom rising above 75 degrees in summer, or going below 45 in winter.

The Purcell House presided over by the genial and jovial Col. J. R. Davis, is one of the best hotels in the country, and affords all the comforts of a home to those desiring to spend a few days in the "City by the Sea."

A new "Shell Road" has been completed to the "Sound," distant six miles, and magnificent carriages, buggies, &c., at reasonable rates can be had to convey the visitor to and from the Ocean over this beautiful "drive." Hundreds of tourists and visitors going to and returning from Florida linger here for weeks loth to leave the delightful climate and the many pleasures that surround them.

An elegant and commodious Union Passenger Depot, in the heart of the city has lately been erected by the W. & W.; &. C. & A. Railroads. It is provided with all modern conveniences. The eating house is one of the best in the southern country, the table being supplied with all the delicacies of the season.

Numerous other places of interest might be mentioned such as the Cotton Factory, employing hundreds of operatives. The cotton compress, which compresses, for shipment to all parts of the civilized world, over 75,000 bales of cotton per year.

The Theatre, one of the prettiest in the South. The Old Brunswick Church, over 100 years old. The magnificent residences with their beautiful lawns dotted with tropical flowers, and the many groves where trees are hung with the celebrated North Carolina Gray Moss.

Purcell House,

WILMINGTON, N. C.

J. R. DAVIS,

PROPRIETOR.

HOW TO GET TO FLORIDA
ALL RAIL.

ATLANTIC COAST LINE.
DAILY ALL RAIL ROUTE No. 1.

Via Richmond, Wilmington, Augusta and Savannah.

Leave New York, 6:00 P. M.; Philadelphia, 8:50 P.M.; Baltimore, 12:05 night; Washington, 1:55 A. M.; Richmond, 7:25 A. M. Pullman Sleeping Cars New York to Richmond. Through train, Parlor Car attached, arriving at Wilmington, N. C., 7:50. P.M.; leave Wilmington, 8:05 P. M. (Pullman Sleeping Car Wilmington to Augusta), arrive Augusta 9:00 A. M. Leave Augusta, 9:30 A. M., via Central Railroad, and 9:30 A. M. Port Royal Railroad, arrive Savannah 5:25 P. M., via Central Railroad, and 4:30 P. M. Port Royal and Savannah and Charleston Railroads; Leave Savannah 4:45 P. M., arrive Jacksonville 11:00 A. M. (Pullman Sleeping Cars Savannah to Jacksonville.)

Aiken passengers connect at Graniteville, 12 miles this side of Augusta, 8:14 A. M., arrive at Aiken, 9:30 A. M.

ATLANTIC COAST LINE.
DAILY ALL RAIL ROUTE No. 2.

Via Richmond, Wilmington, Charleston, and Savannah.

Leave New York 6:00 P. M.; Philadelphia, 8:50 P.M.; Baltimore, 12.05 night; Washingson, 1:55 P. M; Richmond, 7:25 A.M. Pullman Sleeping Cars New York to Richmond. Through train, with parlor cars attached, arriving at Wilmington, 7:50 P. M.; leave Wilmington 8:05 P. M. Pullman Sleeping Car Wilmington to Charleston; arrive Charleston 6:15 A. M.; leave Cnarleston 9:30 A.M.; arrive Savannah 4:30 P. M.; leave Savannah 4:45 P. M.; arrive Jacksonville 11:00 A. M. Pullman Sleeping Cars Savannah to Jacksonville.

ATLANTIC COAST LINE.
DAILY (EXCEPT SUNDAY), ALL RAIL
ROUTE No. 3.

Via Richmond, Wilmington, Charleston and Savannah.

Leave New York, 8:35 A. M.; Philadelphia, 12:15 noon; Baltimore (via Baltimore and Potomac R. R.), 3:40 P. M.; Baltimore (via Baltimore and Ohio R. R.), 4:20 P. M.; Washington, B. and P. R. R. Depot, 6:00 P. M.; Richmond, 11:10 P. M.; Petersburg, 12:20 night; Weldon, 3:45 A. M.; Wilmington, 12:10 noon; Charleston, 11:00 P. M.; Savannah, 8:30 A. M.; arrive Jacksonville, 10:20 P. M.

Parlor Cars to Washington, Pullman Sleeping Cars to Wilmington, Parlor Car to Charleston and Lucas Sleeper to Savannah.

ATLANTIC COAST LINE.
DAILY (EXCEPT SUNDAY), ALL RAIL
ROUTE No. 4.

Via Richmond, Wilmington, Charleston and Savannah.

Leave New York, 9:30 A. M., Limited Express; Philadelphia, 12:13 noon; Baltimore, 2:55 P. M.; arrive Washington, 4:17 P. M. Leave Washington, 6:00 P. M.; Richmond, 11:10 P. M.; Petersburg, 12:20 P. M.; Weldon, 3:45 A. M.; Washington, 12:50 P. M.; Charleston, 11:00 P. M.; Savannah, 8:30 A. M., arrive Jacksonville, 10:20 P. M.

Limited Express is composed entirely of Pullmrn Parlor Cars. Extra from New York to Baltimore, $2.30; New York to Washington, $2.50.

Parlor and sleeping accommodations see Route No. 3.

ROUTE No. 5.

Via Washington, Richmond, Wilmington and Augusta.

Leave New York daily, 6:00 P. M.; Philadelphia, 8:50 P. M.; Baltimore, 12:05 A. M.; Washington, 1:55 A. M.; arrive Richmond, 7:05 A. M. (Pullman Sleeper, New York to Richmond), leave 7:25 A. M. Through train to Wilmington with parlor car attached, arrive Wilmington, 7:50 P. M.; leave 8:05 P. M. Pullman Sleeping Cars to

Augusta, arrive at Augusta, 9:00 A. M.; leave 9:30 A. M.; arrive Macon, 6:25 P. M., there connect with 7:15 P. M., and 3:45 A. M. trains to Jacksonville, via Jesup and Live Oak, arrive at Jacksonville, 10:20 p. m.

ROUTE No. 6.
Via Cumberland Route.

Arrive at Macon as in Atlantic Coast Line Route, No. 5, and Leave 7:15 P. M. Arrive at Brunswick, 6:40 A. M.; leave on Steamer 7:00 A. M. Leave Fernandina, 12:15 noon. Arrive Jacksonville, 2:15 P. M. Leave Macon, 3:45 A. M. Arrive Brunswick. Leave on Steamer 3:00 P. M. Leave Fernandina, 7:15 P. M. Arrive Jacksonville, 10:20 P. M. Elegant Pullman Lucas and Woodruff Sleeping Cars run on the above trains from Macon to Jesup and Brunswick.

DAILY (EXCEPT SUNDAY) BAY LINE ROUTE No. 1.
Via Baltimore, Portsmouth, Wilmington, Charleston and Savannah.

Leave New York 8:40 A. M.; Philadelphia, 12:15 P. M.; Baltimore 4:00 P. M.; steamer arrive Portsmouth 7:00 A. M., in time to connect with through train, with parlor car attached; arrive at Wilmington 7:50 P. M.; thence, same as Route (Atlantic Coast Line) No. 2.

DAILY (EXCEPT SUNDAY) BAY LINE ROUTE No. 2.
Via Baltimore, Portsmouth, Wilmington, Aiken, Augusta and Savannah to Jacksonville, &c., &c.

Leave New York, 8:40 A. M.; Philadelphia, 12:15 P. M.; Baltimore, 4:00 P. M. Steamer arrive at Portsmouth, 7:00 A. M., connecting with through train with Parlar attached for Wilmington, arriving there at 7:50 P. M.; thence as (Atlantic Coast Line) Route No. 1. *Limited Express* leaving New York daily (except Sunday), 9:30 A. M.; Philadelphia, 12:10 noon; arrive at Baltimore, 2:55 P. M. (extra fare, $2.30), connecting with Bay Line Steamers as Nos. 1 and 2 Bay Line Routes.

OLD DOMINION STEAMSHIP ROUTE TO FLORIDA AND THE SOUTH.

The Old Dominion fleet of Passenger Steamers comprised of the following Magnificent Sidewheel Steamships:

Wyanoke, 2,020 tons, (Tuesday), Capt. COUCH.
Isaac Bell, 1,600 tons (Thursday), Capt. LAWRENCE.
Old Dominion, 2,240 tons (Saturday), Capt. WALKER.

Meals and state-room accommodations (included in all through tickets on steamers) are equal to any first-class Hotel or Restaurant.

Time from *New York* to *Norfolk* or *Portsmouth* 25 *hours.*

Baggage checked to all the principal points south.

Leave New York, Pier 37 North River, 3 P. M. Steamer sailing every Tuesday, Thursday, and Saturday; arrive at Portsmouth, Va., 4:00 P. M. following day. Through train leave Portsmsuth 7:00 A. M. (Parlor Car attached), arrive Wilmington 7:50 P. M.; thence same as Atlantic Coast Line Route Nos. 1 and 2.

Through tickets sold, and information given at the Company's various agencies, or at the
General Office of the Company,
197 GREENWICH ST., Cor. of Fulton St., N. Y.
W. H. STANFORD, Sec'y.

Daily Line to Cresent City.

The elegant Steamer **Hampton** connects daily at Palatka with Steamer **Euphemia, for Cresent City,** leaving Jacksonville at 9 A. M., and arriving at Cresent City same day. Through tickets issued by agents o HAMPTON and EUPHEMIA.

No charge for transferring baggage from boats to Hack line.

All Freight shipped by HAMPTON go through from Jacksonville to Cresent City at usual rates, daily.

Easy Hacks run from Cresent City to the **Halifax River,** every Tuesday and Saturday. Tourists will find this the shortest, cheapest and quickest route to Halifax.

JOSEHH W. GARDINER, Secretary,
W. H. CHASE, Ticket Agent, 3 Bay St.   Florida In. Nav. Co.

TRAVELERS' GUIDE TO THE
SOUTH
VIA PIEDMONT AIR LINE.
C. Yingling, Gen. Eastern Agent, 9 Astor House.

ROUTE NO. 1, All Rail via Richmond, Charlotte and Atlanta.

Leave New York at 6:00 P. M., with Pullman Palace Sleeping Cars and first-class Passenger Cars through to Belle Isle Junction (opposite Richmond,) without change.

Leave West Philadelphia Depot, 8:50 P. M.

Leave Charles Street Depot, Baltimore, at 12:05 A. M. A Sleeping Car for Richmond without change, leave Calvert Station, Baltimore, which passengers can occupy as early as 9:00 P. M.

Leave Washington 1:55 A. M. Arrive at Richmond 7:05 A. M. Leave Richmond, via Richmond and Danville R. R. at 7:30 A. M. Leave Belle Isle Junction at 8.22 A. M. (Breakfast). Via Piedmont Air Line, R. & D. R. R. and A. & R. A. L. Railway and connections on train with Palace Sleeping Cars, and new first-class Parlor Cars attached. The Sleeping Cars run through to Brunswick, Ga , 836 miles, without change, from Richmond, via Atlanta. Another Sleeping Car being attached to train at Atlanta for New Orleans, makes practically but one change of cars from New York to New Orleans by this route. Leave Danville at 2:55 P. M.—Dinner. Leave Greensboro 5:40 P. M Arrive at Salisbury 7:55 P. M.—Supper. Arrive at Charlotte 10:37 P. M. Arrive Greenville 3:04 A. M. Arrive at Buford 8:05 A. M.—Breakfast. Arrive at Atlanta 10:15 A. M. Six hours better time than by any other line, only 40 hours from New York to Atlanta. Arrive at Opelika 6:29 P. M. Arrive at Columbus 10:00 P. M. Arrive at Montgomery 9:30 P. M. Mobile 4:10 A. M. Arrive New Orleans 10:00 A. M., making close connection for Galveston, Texas. Arriving next day at 11:00 A. M. *QUICKEST TIME MADE—ONLY 64 HOURS NEW YORK TO NEW ORLEANS*, and 89 hours to Galveston. 48 hours to Macon.

FOR FLORIDA,
Leave Richmond 7:30 A. M., Belle Isle Junction 8:22

A. M. in through Palace Sleeping Car to Brunswick, Ga., 836 miles without change, Arrive at Atlanta 10:15 A. M. Arrive at Macon 6:00 P. M. Arrive Brunswick, Ga., at 6:30 A. M. Thence by steamer, inside route, Breakfast on Boat, a beautiful run of $3\frac{1}{2}$ hours, Arriving at Fernandia 10:30 A. M. Leave Fernandia via rail without change of cars and Arrive at Jacksonville at 2 00 P. M., only 68 hours New York to Jacksonville, and with less changes of cars than via any other route.

ROUTE NO. 2, All Rail via Richmond, Charlotte and Columbia.

. Leave New York, Philadelphia, Baltimore, Washington and Richmond as in schedule route No. 1. Arrive at Salisbury 7:55 P. M.—Supper, and leave at 8:15 P. M., in through Sleeping Car to Augusta without change. Arrive at Columbia 5:10 A. M. Arrive at Graniteville 8:14 A. M. Arrive at Aiken 9:30 A. M. Arrive at Augusta 9:00 A M. Arrive at Savannah 4:30 P. M., via Port Royal R. R., via the Central R. R. of Ga. at 5:25 P. M. Leave Savannah at 4;45 P. M., with through Sleeping Cars without change, and arrive in Jacksonville at 10.55 A. M., only 64 hours Ne 7 York to Jacksonville. Quickest time ever made and less changes of Cars. Practically but *ONE CHANGE* of Cars from *NEW YORK* to *AUGUSTA*. Arrive at Macon 6.35 P. M, Only $39\frac{1}{2}$ hours New York to Augusta, and 46 hours to Savannah. *ASK FOR TICKETS* via this Route, by *RICHMOND, CHARLOTTE* and *AUGUSTA*.

Virginia Midland Route.
G. M. Huntington, Agent. 315 Broadway, N. Y.

Via Danville, Atlanta, Brunswick, Fernandina. Leave New York 6.00 P. M.; sleeping car to Danville. Leave Philadelphia 8.50 P. M., Baltimore 12.05 P. M., Washington 2.10 A. M., Charlottesville 1.55 P.M. Arrive at Gordonsville 6.55 A. M., (breakfast). Arrive at Lynchburg 11.07 A. M. Arrive at Dundee (Danville Junction) 2.30 P. M., (dinner;) change. Take through sleeping car to Brunswick. Arrive 6.30 A. M. Leave via boat to Fernandina 7.00 A. M. Arrive at Fernandina 11. A. M. Cars to Jacksonville. Arrive 2.15 P. M.

NEW YORK AND SAVANNAH STEAMSHIP LINE.

The Sea routes from New York to Savannah are composed of the most finely appointed steamers on the Atlantic coast, and comprise the following steamships:

Gen. Barnes and Herman Livingston, sailing alternately, Tuesdays, from Pier 43 North River, at 3:00 P. M., GEORGE YONGE, Agent, 409 Broadway; Magnolia and Rapidan, alternately, from Pier 16 East River, Thursdays, at 3:00 P. M., MURRAY, FERRIS & Co., Agents; San Salvador and San Jacinto, sailing Saturdays, alternately, from Pier 43 North River, GEORGE YONGE, Agent, 409 Broadway, New York.

From Savannah to Jacksonville, Inside Route.—The elegant, fast and Commodious steamer J. B. Schuyler will leave Savannah twice a week for Jacksonville, making connections with New York and Savannah steamships, and ALL RAIL ROUTES both ways.

HUNTER & GAMMELL, Agents, Savannah, Ga.

NEW YORK AND CHARLESTON STEAMSHIP COMPANY'S LINE.

Great Southern Freight and Passenger Route, via Charleston. Favorite Route to Florida.

One of the following elegant and well-known Steamships is appointed to sail every Wednesday and Saturday, from Pier 29 North River, 3 P. M. : City of Atlanta, Capt. M. S. Woodhull. Cleopatra, Capt. Bulkley. Champion, Capt. R. W. Lockwood. G. W. Clyde, Capt. Ingrahm.

The above steamers have been handsomely fitted up for the convenience of passengers, and are unrivaled on the coast for Safety, Speed and Comfort. Excursion Tickets at reduced rates, apply to

BENTLY D. HAZEL, Gen'l Agt. 317 Broadway, N. Y.

W. P. CLYDE & Co., No. 6 Bowling Green.

J W. QUINTARD & Co.. Agts., 177 West St., N. Y.

PIEDMONT AIR LINE.

ROUTE No. 1.

All Rail via Richmond, Charlotte and Atlanta.

ONLY 68 HOURS, NEW YORK TO JACKSONVILLE.
Pullman Palace Sleeping Cars, and First-Class Passenger Cars run Through.

New York to Richmond without Change.
PALACE SLEEPING CARS.

RICHMOND TO BRUNSWICK, GA.,
836 Miles, without Change.

This route now offers the most comfortable arrangements and and Perfect Schedules, with through cars, &c., that has ever been enjoyed by visitors to Florida and the South.

EQUIPMENT NEW and FIRST-CLASS in all its appointments.

PALACE SLEEPING and PARLOR CARS, and SUPERB DAY COACHES, with all modern improvements, Automatic Air Brakes, &c.

Practically, but one change of cars New York to New Orleans, Jacksonville, or Augusta.

EXCURSION TICKETS

Via this Route to Jacksonville good to return on till May 31st, 1877, at *greatly reduced rates.*

ROUTE No. 2.

All Rail via Richmond, Charlotte and Columbia.

Leave New York, Philadelphia, Baltimore, Washington and Richmond as in Schedule Route No. 1. Arrive at Salisbury 7:55 P. M.—Supper—and leave at 8:15 P. M., in through Sleeping Car to Augusta without change. Arrive at Columbia 5:10 A. M. Arrive at Graniteville 8:14 A. M. Arrive at Aiken 9:30 A.M. Arrive at Augusta 9:00 A.M Arrive at Savannah 4:30 P. M., via Port Royal R.R., via the Central R.R. of Georgia, at 5:25 P.M. Leave Savannah at 4:45 P.M., with Through Sleeping Cars, without change, and arrive at Jacksonville at 10:55 A.M., *only 64 Hours New York to Jacksonville.*

Be sure and get your Tickets via Richmond, Greensboro' and Atlanta.

C. YINGLING,
Gen. Eastern Passenger Agent, 9 Astor House.

J. R. MACMURDO,
Gen. Passenger Agent, Richmond, Va.

THE Atlantic Coast Line of Railways.

ALL RAIL ROUTE TO
Charleston, Savannah, Jacksonville,
AND ALL POINTS IN
FLORIDA,
—VIA—
Washington, Richmond & Wilmington

The Transportation arrangements of this Line for the Fall and Winter busiuess of 1876-7 have been perfected with reference to the requisite accommodation in a first-class manner of all Southern-bound travel.

Double Daily Trains are run between
Washington and Jacksonville via Charleston,
Giving close connections with all lines North thereof.

And the Schedule Time between NEW YORK and CHARLESTON has been quickened to an extent never before attempted.

Through Pullman Sleeping Cars and Atlantic Coast Line Parlor Cars,

Are run between all prominent points on this route, and in such unbroken manner as commends the line above all others to invalids and families.

Baggage Checked Through. Tickets Good Until Used,
With privilege of stopping off at all terminal points.

THROUGH TICKETS

Sold throughout the East to all points South via this line and all information given at the principal Railroad offices, North and South.

JONAH H. WHITE, Southern Passenger Agent.

General Office, No. 229 Broadway, New York,
Will answer all communications addressed to him.

W. J. WALKER,　　　　**A. POPE,**
General Agent.　　　　Gen. Pass. & Ticket Agent

FAVORITE FLORIDA ROUTE
VIA
Baltimore, Portsmouth and Wilmington,
Popularly known to the traveling public as the
BAY LINE ROUTE.
Persons visiting FLORIDA should remember that the
Bay Line of Steamers
Is one of the oldest and best managed lines in the South. The steamers of this Line are the Largest, Fastest and Most Elegant South of New York.

LEAVING DAILY (Sunday Excepted)
FROM BALTIMORE
on the arrival of the Morning Train from
NEW YORK, and noon train from PHILADELPHIA.

A Section of the Steamers with State Rooms, Berths, &c., is reserved exclusively for Ladies and Children traveling alone.

Passengers arrive at
PORTSMOUTH
In time to take the through train to
Wilmington (Without Change,)
Connecting with
PULLMAN PALACE SLEEPING CARS
FOR
CHARLESTON AND AUGUSTA,
Connecting at both the above points with throught trains for
Savannah and all Points in Florida.

The Meals furnished are unequalled; having access to the markets of Baltimore and Norfolk, unquestionably the best in the country.

☞ **Supper and Breakfast and an entire Night's Rest on the Bay Line Steamers.**

Baggage Checked Through to all the principal points.

Persons returning north will find Schedule, &c., &c., equally as perfect as going south.

Tickets good until used, with the privilege of stopping over at all Terminal Points, can be obtained at all Principal Ticket Offices, North and South. SCHEDULES giving time and all necessary information can be obtained wherever Through Tickets are sold.

W. J. WALKER,   **EMMET BROWN,**
General Passenger Agent.   General Ticket Agent.

H. V. TOMPKINS, Southern Passenger Agent.

The Atlantic & Gulf
FREIGHT AND PASSENGER LINE
VIA SAVANNAH, GA., TO ALL POINTS IN
Florida, Southern and Middle Georgia,
FLINT, APALACHICOLA AND CHATTAHOOCHEE RIVERS,

Fast Freight Express, via Savannah Steamships, to Savannah, Ga., and Atlantic & Gulf; Macon & Brunswick; Jacksonville, Pensacola & Mobile Rail Roads.

AND CONNECTING LINES.

Pullman's Palace Sleeping Cars on all Night Trains.

TWO TRAINS DAILY FROM SAVANNAH

to JACKSONVILLE, connecting with Steamers on ST. JOHN'S RIVER, for St. Augustine, Palatka, Green Cove Springs, Hibernia, Orange Mills, Enterprise, etc., etc.

Shippers are requested to mark all packages—"Care of ATLANTIC AND GULF R. R. Agent, SAVANNAH, Ga.," and to so state it on Ship's Receipt and Bill of Lading.

Freight Received and Through Bills of Lading issued by Agents of the Line as follows:

BOSTON TO SAVANNAH, GA.

DIRECT—The Steamers SEMINOLE and SOMERSET leave on the 10th, 20th and 30th of each month. F. NICKERSON & CO., Agents, 205 State St., Boston
A. M. BOCK, General Agent, Jacksonville, Fla.

BOSTON via NEW YORK TO SAVANNAH, GA.

Ship daily, via of BOSTON, AND PROVIDENCE R. R. and PROVIDENCE AND NEW YORK STEAMSHIP CO., or OLD COLONY R. R.
GEO. C. MORRILL, Agent, 77 Washington St., Boston.

NEW YORK TO SAVANNAH, GA.
THREE DEPARTURES PER WEEK

Ships Rapidan and Magnolia, Sailing Thursdays from Pier 16 East River. Office, Nos. 60 and 62 South Street.
Ships San Salvador, San Jacinto, Herman Livingston, and General Barnes, Sailing Thursdays and Saturdays, from Pier 43 North River. Office, No. 409 Broadway, New York.

PHILADELPHIA TO SAVANNAH, GA.

The PHILADELPHIA AND SOUTHERN STEAMSHIP CO. despatch one of their Steamers, Wyoming or Juniata, every Saturday. Returning, leave Savannah same day. W. L. James, Agent, 46 South Delaware Ave., Phila.

BALTIMORE TO SAVANNAH, GA.

The AMERICA, SARAGOSSA AND NORTH POINT, leave on 10th, 20th and 30th of each month. A. L. HUGGINS, Long Dock Wharf, Baltimore.
Information given and tickets sold to all points in Florida, in connection with the "Atlantic and Gulf Railway." C. D. OWENS, Gen'l Ag't, 315 Broadway, N.Y

For Florida, and all Points South and South-West.

THE GREAT SOUTHERN
Freight and Passenger Route.
—VIA—
New York and Savannah Steamship Line.

One of the following first-class side-wheel steamships will sail as follows, punctually, at 3 o'clock, P. M.:

EVERY TUESDAY—H. LIVINGSTON, Capt. MALLORY; or GEN. BARNES, Capt. CHEESEMAN, from Pier 43 North River. GEORGE YONGE, Agent, 409 Broadway.

EVERY THURSDAY.—MAGNOLIA, Capt. DAGGETT; or RAPIDAN, Capt. KEMPTON, from Pier 16 East River, foot of Wall St. MURRAY, FERRIS & Co., Agents, 62 South St.

EVERY SATURDAY.—SAN SALVADOR, Capt. NICKERSON; or SAN JACINTO, Capt. HAZARD, from Pier 43 North River. GEORGE YONGE, Agent, 409 Broadway.

Connecting at Savannah, Ga., with **CENTRAL RAILROAD.**

Two trains daily for all points in Middle, North, and South-West Georgia, Alabama, Mississippi, Tennessee and Louisiana, and with the **ATLANTIC AND GULF RAILROAD,** to all points in Florida, Southern and Middle Georgia, and with steamers in the Chattahoochee River. Two fast trains daily between Savannah and Jacksonville, Fla. Pullman's Palace Sleeping Cars and elegant Parlor Coaches attached to both trains.

Tickets for St. John's River and St. Augustine also good by Steamboats from Savannah.

These fine steamers, on this favorite line of travel to the South are newly and handsomely fitted up for the comfort and convenience of passengers; have large carrying capacity; and are of sufficient light draft of water *to insure no detention* in the Savannah River.

Families *en route* for Florida, Georgia Alabama, and even as far New Orleans will find the Savannah route the most enjoyable, for comfort as well as saving in expense.

The Florida Steamers leave Savannah three days in the week, for all points on the coast.

Through Bills of Lading given for freights to all points in FLORIDA, GEORGIA, ALABAMA, and TENNESSEE. Rates and Classifications will be furnished by the undersigned:

Shippers may feel assured of no delay to their goods in being forwarded, and as the increase of trade demands, additional steamers, equally suitable to all the requirements, will be placed on the route.

Goods forwarded through New York and Savannah *Free of Commission.*

Freight received daily at the Covered **Pier 43 North River,** and **Pier 16 East River.**

For Freight or passage by ships sailing on Thursdays, from Pier 16 East River, apply to

MURRAY, FERRIS & CO., Agents, 62 South St.

For Freight or Passage by ships sailing from Pier 43 North River, on Tuesdays and Saturdays, apply to

GEORGE YONGE, Agent, 409 Broadway.

NEW LINE TO & FROM FLORIDA.
The Cumberland Route.

Comfort, Speed and Attractiveness Combined. The Shortest Line to and from Jacksonville. New Fast Double Daily Line to and from Florida.

The Macon & Brunswick R. R., in connection with the Atlantic, Gulf & West India Transit Co. will open, on and after December 1st, 1876, a new line to and from Florida, by way of Macon, Jesup, Brunswick, Fernandina, Baldwin and Jacksonville. The steamer between Brunswick and Fernandina is first-class in all her appointments, and the run is all daylight or comparatively early evening.

The table on the boat will be unsurpassed and "*a la carte.*" The navigation is entirely inland along the attractive sea island, and sometimes in view of the ocean. Time on the steamer, between three and four hours. The connections at Atlanta, Augusta and Macon are complete. Fare same as by any other route. Baggage checked through, or checks exchanged by baggage masters, without disturbance to the passengers. The change from an all rail trip to and from Florida to one with above amount of water, will, it is believed, afford rest, refreshment and attractiveness. Where one, however, prefers all rail, the other route to and from Florida, via Macon, Jesup, Live Oak and Jacksonville is open to them. No change of cars between Fernandina and Jacksonville. The Cumberland Route is, as between the common points Jesup and Jacksonville, fifty-eight miles shorter than any other route, and as between the common points Jacksonville, Florida and Nashville, Tennessee, is forty-six miles the shortest. Palace Sleeping Cars on all night trains.

Straight, Excursion and Tourists' Tickets on sale at all principal ticket offices. Ask for tickets by the Cumberland Route, and take no other. For schedules and further particulars see small bills, or address either

H. M. DRANE, G. T. & P. Agt. M. & B. R. R., Macon, Ga.
A. O. MacDonell, G. T. Agt., A. G. & Wt. In. I. Co., Fernandina. Fla.
Capt. A. A. SHARP, Gen. Traveling Agt., Jacksonville, Fla.

TO AND FROM

FLORIDA AND THE NORTH

—VIA—

OLD DOMINION LINE

OF STEAMERS

AND THE

Atlantic Coast Line of Railways.

Elegant Side-Wheel Passenger Steamers.

OLD DOMINION, - - - **2222 Tons.**
WYANOKE, - - - - 2067 "
ISAAC BELL, - - - - 1600 "

The Steamers are the largest and most comfortable sailing out of New York.

Leaving Pier 37 Noth River, Foot of Beach Street,

EVERY TUESDAY, THURSDAY AND SATURDAY,

At 3 O'Clock, P. M.

The Steamers Leave NORFOLK

EVERY MONDAY, WEDNESDAY AND SATURDAY,

At 7:30 P. M., on the arrival of the southern trains.

Only 26 hours Sea Voyage by this line, avoiding exposure along the Coast of **Cape Hatteras**, &c. Time through from all Points South and Southwest to **New York**, within 4 hours of all the Rail Routes.

Tickets by this Route include Meals and State Room accommodations on Steamers.

BAGGAGE CHECKED THROUGH.

For Tickets, Time Cards, and full information apply at

OLD DOMINION S. S. CO.,

197 GREENWICH STREET,

Or 229 Broadway.

ATLANTIC COAST LINE.

A. POPE,   **W. H. STANFORD,**
Gen. Pass. Agt. Atlantic Coast Line.   Sec'y O. D. S. S. CO.

EXCURSION TICKETS

TO FLORIDA

ARE NOW ON SALE, EXCLUSIVELY, BY THE

Virginia Midland Road

AND ITS CONNECTIONS,

Giving the passenger the option of going by Lynchburg, Knoxville, and Atlanta, or by Danville, Charlotte, Atlanta, and Macon.

These Tickets can also be used either by rail from Jesup, Ga., to Jacksonville, or by water from Brunswick, Ga., to Fernandina (the new Cumberland Route.)

The Virginia Midland

Offers the greatest variety of "straight" tickets to Florida and all Southern points.

Palace Cars through from Boston to Danville, from Washington to Atlanta, from Danville to Brunswick, and from Atlanta to Jacksonville.

Quick time—Close connections. Trains double daily over most of the distance.

Purchase tickets by the **Virginia Midland.**

G. M. HUNTINGTON,

Gen'l Eastern Agent,
315 Broadway, New York.

THE PREFERRED ROUTE TO FLORIDA

IS VIA THE

Atlantic & Gulf Railroad

FROM

SAVANNAH, JESUP, OR ALBANY, GA.

Avoiding sea-sickness and the detention of Steamer Lines at the John's River Bar.

Two Fast Trains Daily between Savannah & Jacksonville.

LEAVE SAVANNAH	8:30 A.M.	(Sundays excepted).	
ARRIVE JACKSONVILLE	10:10 P.M.	"	"
LEAVE SAVANNAH	4:45 P.M.	Daily.	
ARRIVE JACKSONVILLE	11:00 A.M.	"	
" TALLAHASSEE	8:35 A.M.	"	

The Morning Train from Savannah connects with all Northern Trains, and with the M. & B. R. R. Train at Jesup,

The Evening Train connects with Northern Trains via Augusta and Yemassee only.

Lucas Drawing Room Cars, especially arranged for the convenience of invalids, are attached to the Day Trains. Also through Pullman Sleeping Cars from Louisville, Ky., to Jacksonville via Jesup.

The 4:45 P.M. Train makes close connection with Steamers on St. John's River.

No omnibus transfer between the Savannah & Charleston and A. & G. Railroads at Savannah.

Good Eating Houses at regular intervals.

For further information apply to

GEO. S. HAINES,
General Ticket Agent,
SAVANNAH, GA.

C. D. OWENS,
General Agent,
315 BROADWAY, NEW YORK.

Boston & New York Air Line R. R.

VIA NEW HAVEN, MIDDLETOWN AND WILLIMANTIC.

THE
SHORTEST ALL RAIL ROUTE

Between NEW YORK and

MIDDLETOWN, WILLIMANTIC, LOWELL, NASHUA, WORCESTER, FITCHBURG, CONCORD, **BOSTON** PORTLAND, AUGUSTA, BANGOR, ETC.

SECURE YOUR TICKETS VIA AIR LINE R. R.

NEW YORK DEPOT, Grand Central Depot, 42d St. and 4th Ave.

J. E. FOSTER, Gen'l Pass. Ag't, 347 Broadway, N. Y.

W. H. TURNER, Supt., New Haven, Ct.

WINTER RESORT,
FERNANDINA, FLA.

MANSION HOUSE

Accommodation for 150 Guests.

With a shell road to the finest beach on the Atlantic coast, making a drive of twenty miles, and water for sailing and fishing, and a clear, brilliant climate.

FERNANDINA

Stands Unrivalled as a Resort for Sportsmen and Yachtsmen.

Ladies will also find a luxurious winter home in the midst of an orange grove and the rarest roses.

Table Furnished from the New York Market
BY STEAMERS.

M. W. DOWNIE, Proprietor.

QUICK DISPATCH, SAFETY & COMFORT.

THE
New Orleans, Florida and Havana
STEAMSHIP CO.

Will dispatch one of their first-class U. S. Mail Steamers from New Orleans and Havana

EVERY WEDNESDAY,

Touching at Cedar Keys and Key West, and connecting with Steamers for Apalachicola, St. Mark's, Tampa, and the Suwanee River.

These Steamers are first-class—have good passenger accommodations—are kept in good condition, and are commanded by careful and experienced officers, who make every effort for the safety, comfort and pleasure of travelers.

The advantages to travelers seeking safety, comfort and pleasure on a steamship, are apparent in selecting this route, as rough sea is almost unknown in these waters.

RATES OF FIRST-CLASS PASSAGE.

FROM	TO								
	New Orl'ns	Cedar Keys	Tampa	Key West	Havana	Jack's'n'ill'	Fer'n'n'i'a	Charleston	Savan'h
New Orleans	..	$25	$35	$40	$40	$31	$31	$35	$35
Cedar Keys	$25		10	20	25	..	..	..	..
Tampa	35	10	..	25	35	16	16	25	25
Key West	40	20	25	..	12	26	26	32	32
Havana	40	25	35	12	..	26	26	35	35
Jacksonville	31	..	16	26	26	..	..	..	..
Fernandina	31	..	16	26	26	..	..	..	..
Charleston	35	..	..	32	35	..	..	..	..
Savannah	35	..	..	32	35	..	..	..	..

For further information apply to

Atlantic, Gulf & West India Transit Company	Fernandina, Fla.
Florida Central Railroad Co.	Jacksonville, "
E. J. Lutterloh	Cedar Keys, "
Miller & Henderson	Tampa, "
Jno. Jay Philbrick	Key West, "
Ravenel & Co.	Charleston, S. C
Agents Florida Steam Packet Co.	Savannah, Ga.
Lawton Bros., 13 Mercaderes Street	Havana, Caba.

I. K. ROBERTS,
120 Common St., New Orleans, La.

Savannah & Charleston
RAILROAD.

ONLY ROUTE THROUGH CITY OF SAVANNAH HAVING NO OMNIBUS TRANSFER.

Shortest, Most Comfortable, and Only Direct Route to ALL POINTS IN FLORIDA.

30 Miles Shorter than any other Route.

Double Daily Trains, Carrying the U. S. Mails.

PULLMAN CARS ON THE ENTIRE ROUTE

S. C. BOYLSTON,
   G. F. & T. Agent.

C. S. GADSDEN,
   General Superintendent.

St. John's River Schedule.

BROCK & COXETTER'S DAILY LINE.

THROUGH STEAMERS
Daily except Sunday.
Leave Jacksonville..11:00 A.M.
Arrive Tocoi........ 3:20 P.M.
Leave   "   .... 3:25 "
Arrive St. Augustine. 4:15 "
   "   Palatka...... 6:30 "
   "   Enterprise (next day) 10:00 A.M.

THROUGH STEAMERS
Daily except Sunday.
Leave St. Augustine.. 5:00 A.M.
   "   Palatka....... 6:00 P.M.
   "   St. Augustine. 4:45 "
   "   Tocoi·........ 7:30 "
Arrive Jacksonville..11:00 "

WAY STEAMERS.
Daily Except Sunday.
Leave Jacksonville...2:00 P.M.
Arrive Tocoi........5:30 "
   "   St. Augustine..8:15 "
   "   Palatka........7:30 "

WAY STEAMERS.
Daily Except Sunday.
Leave Palatka....... 7:00 A.M
   "   St. Augustine.. 7:55 "
   "   Tocoi.......... 8:20 "
Arrive Jacksonville..,12:30 P.M

THE MAGNOLIA
Passenger Route
—VIA—
AUGUSTA & PORT ROYAL R. R.
—TO—
SAVANNAH, Ga., AND FLORIDA.

THE ONLY LINE via Augusta connecting with the ATLANTIC & GULF RAILROAD at Savannah, avoiding the *long, tedious* and well-known omnibus transfer through that city.

THE ONLY LINE via Augusta offering *Close Double Daily All Rail Connections* between Augusta and Jacksonville, Florida.

THE ONLY LINE via Augusta running *Pullman Palace Sleeping Cars* between Augusta and Savannah, Ga.

THE ONLY LINE via Augusta, running *Through Day Coaches* between Augusta and Savannah, Ga., thus avoiding disagreeable changes, at midway stations, incident to other lines.

Passengers by the following favorite routes to Savannah, Ga., and Florida—**Atlantic Coast Line, Piedmont Air Line, Virginia Midland Route**—will please *see that their tickets read* " via *Augusta and Yemassee.*"

Baggage Checked through and Tickets on Sale at all Offices where those of the Pennsylvania and Baltimore & Ohio Railroads are sold.

Further information given upon application to

T. S. DAVANT,
General Freight and Pass. Agent,
AUGUSTA, GA.

R. H. THAYER, Gen'l Ag't,
263 Broadway, New York.

THE HYGEIA HOTEL, OLD POINT COMFORT, VA.

THE HYGEIA HOTEL, - - Old Point Comfort, Va.

This Hotel, thoroughly built and comfortably furnished, will be opened for the reception of Guests all the year.

It is situated on the beach and at the head of the landing for the various steamers that touch at Old Point Comfort.

It can be reached tri-weekly by the elegant steamships of the Old Dominion Steamship Company of New York, or by rail from that city and Philadelphia to Baltimore, and thence by the splendid steamers of the Old Bay Line. Daily facilities of the same character from Washington via Baltimore, and semi-weekly from Washington direct by Steamer Jane Mosley. From Richmond and Petersburg a daily communication also is had by the fine steamers upon the river, and by the Atlantic, Mississippi and Ohio Railroad and Bay Line Steamers from Norfolk. An almost hourly communication is had with Norfolk by steamers touching at the pier on their way to and from New York, Baltimore, Washington, Richmond, Petersburg, Yorktown, Matthews, Cherrystone, Cobb's Island, Vue de l'Eau, Hampton and Smithfield, Va.

As a resort for the pleasure seeker or invalid and a resting place for tourists to and from Florida, this Hotel offers inducements certainly not exceeded by any point on the Atlantic coast.

The drives in the vicinity are delightful, the Hampton Normal and Agricultural School, the National Military Home, the National Cemetery, and the Town of Hampton—containing one of the oldest churches in the country—all are within the limits of an easy ride, drive, or sail.

Fortress Monroe, now become classic to Americans generally, is within a minute's walk, always open to visitors, and is another grand feature in the pleasure of a visit to this locality; it is the largest in America, and the parade grounds within it delightfully shaded with live oaks. The famed Artillery School has its establishment within the Fortress, and the dress parade, with the music of a fine band, morning and evening, with open air concerts given by the band Monday, Wednesday, and Friday Evenings, gives the visitor pleasure rarely or never found at the seaside or any resort.

In the the management of the Hotel every effort will be made to secure the comfort and pleasure of the Guests, and to make it in every way worthy of their patronage. The table will be furnished in abundance with every delicacy of the season. Bathing, boating and fishing facilites will also be provided, and those pleasures can have no better locality for their enjoyment.

The climate during the year is unsurpassed for salubrity, the range of the thermometer here for the past 10 years, as taken from the notes of the Meteorological Observatory shows an average of 60°, 74°, 76° for Summer; 70°, 59°, 46° for Autumn; 45°, 44°, 42° for Winter; 48°, 52°, 63° for Spring months.

TERM: Transient, $3.00 per day, $17.00 per week and upwards, according to location, &c.

For further information, address,

H. PHOEBUS, Proprietor,

THE HYGEIA HOTEL, OLD POINT COMFORT, VA.

NASSAU, N. P. BAHAMAS,
A FAMOUS WINTER RESORT.
ROYAL VICTORIA HOTEL.

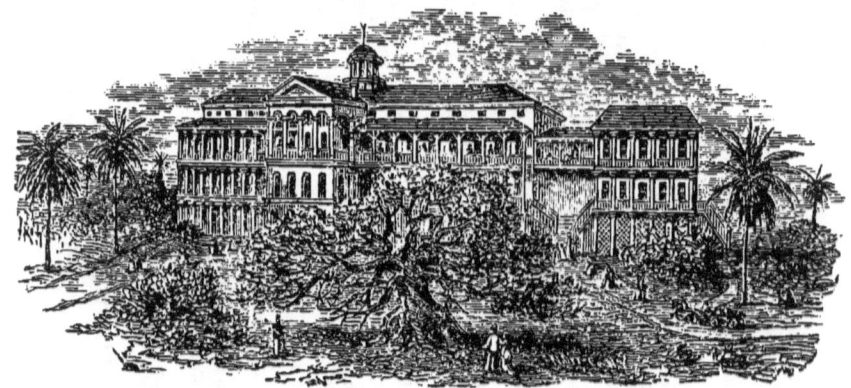

FIRST-CLASS MAIL AND PASSENGER STEAMSHIPS
Under contract with the Bahamas Government, leave

New York & Savannah,
EVERY TEN DAYS.

Making close connections at **Savannah** with **First-Class Steamers** to and from **New York**, or by *Rail* to all parts of the country, thus giving the option of a short sea voyage to or from **Savannah**, or a longer voyage to or from **New York**; also affording to invalids seeking a **more equable climate** than **Florida** can offer, **Nassau** is particularly recommended, where the **temperature never falls below 64°** **Fahrenheit, nor rises above 82°**, and where the variation does not exceed 5° in 24 hours.

For Illustrated Nassau Guides and Schedules giving full particulars, address,

MURRAY, FERRIS & CO., Or **HUNTER & GAMMELL,**
62 South St., N. Y.   Savannah, Ga.

G. LEVE, Gen'l Passenger Agent, 202 St. James St. Montreal, Canada.
A. M. BOCK, General Agent, Jacksonville, Fla.

THE HIGHLAND PARK HOTEL, Aiken, South Carolina.

The Highland Park Hotel has been enlarged to nearly double its former size, and has accommodation for 250 guests. Rooms are large, with open fireplace, and each have sunny exposure. The broad piazzas and corridors afford a promenade one-quarter of a mile in length. Walks and drives unsurpassed. Public parlor, office and gents' sitting-rooms on first floor (facing the South), electric bells to each room, hot and cold baths on each floor; children's play-room, billiard-room, barber shop, &c., in the basement. well stocked livery stable connected with the Hotel. Grounds ample, with facilities for various amusements. Circulars and rates of board furnished by addressing **B. P. CHATFIELD, Prop'r.**

E. H. TOMLINSON, Manager.

NOTE.—**Planters' Hotel**, Augusta, Ga., refitted and furnished new throughout. Open the whole year. Rooms at Highland Park Hotel can be secured here. **B. P. CHATFIELD, Prop'r.**
B. F. BROWN, Manager.

ATLANTIC HOTEL,

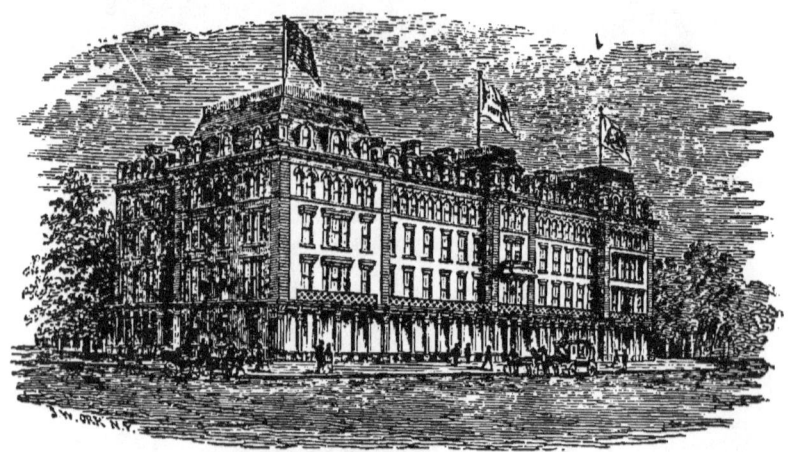

NORFOLK, VA.

R. S. DODSON, - - - Proprietor.

FINE WINTER RESORT.

Board, - - $2.50 and $3.00 per Day.

And Liberal Arrangements by the Week or Month.

Purcell House,

WILMINGTON, N. C.

J. R. DAVIS,

PROPRIETOR.

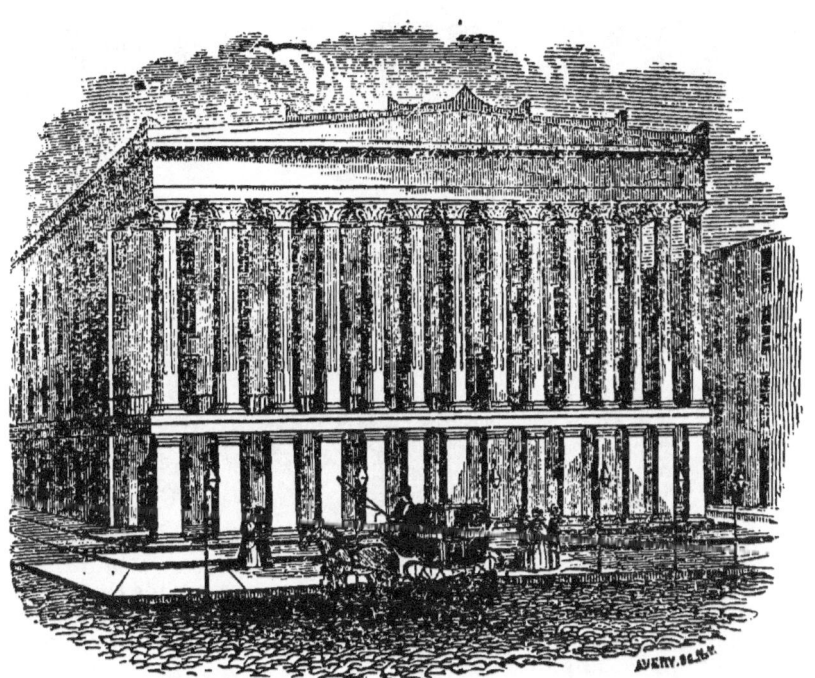

CHARLESTON HOTEL
CHARLESTON, SOUTH CAROLINA.

This well-known and popular first class Hotel, situated in the centre of the city, and also in the centre of the Wholesale Business Houses, affords facilities, comfort, and attention to travellers for pleasure and merchants on business, second to none in the United States

Having been recently thoroughly repaired and newly furnished throughout, the Proprietors pledge themselves to spare no pains in the management to maintain the high reputation heretofore enjoyed by the old "CHARLESTON" as a first-class house.

E. H. JACKSON & CO., Proprietors.

ALTAMAHA HOTEL,
JESUP, GA.

This well-known Hotel, at the Junction of the Atlantic Gulf and Macon and Brunswick Railroads, has passed under the control of the A. & G. R. R. Co., and under the management of Mr. W. G. Norwood, for the past three years manager of the Screven House, Savannah, Ga.

Board by the week or month can be obtained on reasonable terms, upon application to the Manager. All passenger trains on both roads stop here, and allow ample time for meals.

PAVILION HOTEL,
G. T. ALFORD & CO.,
CHARLESTON, S. C.

On and after the 17th day of October, 1876, the transient rate of this well known house will be reduced to suit the times. Board from $2.50 to $3 per day, according to location of rooms. This Hotel has recently been renovated and repainted, and no pains shall be spared to make our guests comfortable and happy. All transfer coupons taken by omnibuses of Pavilion Hotel.

MARSHALL HOUSE, SAVANNAH, GA.
The only Perfect Edifice in the City Originally Built for Hotel Purposes.

It is of modern style of construction, and possesses all the appointments of a first-class establishment, embracing a *cuisine* of superlative excellence, offering superior accommodations at rates reduced to **Three Dollars Per Day.**

A. B. LUCE, Proprietor.

SCREVEN HOUSE.

SAVANNAH, GA.

R. BRADLEY, Proprietor.

Rates, $3.00, per Day.
Special arrangements by the week or month.
GEO. McGINLY, Proprietor.

ST. JAMES HOTEL
JACKSONVILLE, FLORIDA.
J. R. CAMPBELL, MANAGER.
(OPEN FROM NOVEMBER TO MAY.)

THIS FAVORITE HOUSE with accommodations for 300 guests, having been refitted and newly furnished, will open November 25th, 1876, for the reception of Winter guests.

A new Passenger Elevator, one of the best manufacture, has been added the present season.

An Orchestra has been engaged for the season.

Special arrangements will be made for board by the week or the entire season, and rooms may be secured by mail or telegraph.

Jacksonville, Florida.
THE LAND OF FLOWERS.

Stimpson, Devnell & Davis,
PROPRIETORS.

The above cut represents this spacious, new brick hotel, just completed. [G]as in every room; Laundry and Bath Rooms. The house is provided [w]ith Creighton's Oral Enunciator, an Elevator, and is thoroughly finished [th]roughout in first-class style.

The house has been built with especial reference to egress in case of [fi]re, having also stand pipes with line of hose on each floor connected with [th]e same.

The cuisine department has all the modern improvements and is under [ch]arge of a competent person who has had long experience in a leading [B]oston hotel. The is to be kept first-class in every respect.

TREMONT HOUSE.

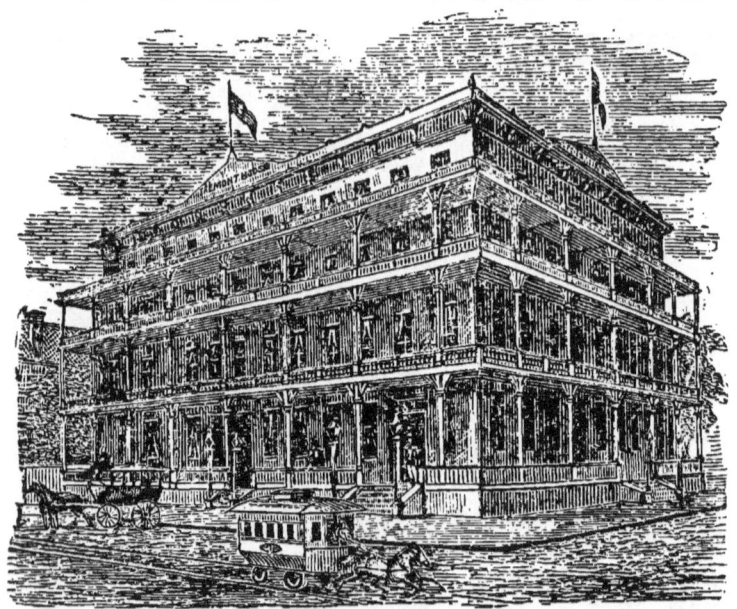

WASHINGTON, D. C.,
Has been Enlarged to accommodate 300 Guests.

Is newly furnished throughout with Superior Furniture, and kept in every respect as a First-Class Hotel.

Our Motto: **A Full House** at a Moderate Price.

Terms, $2.50 per Day.

The Proprietor runs his own omnibuses to all trains and steamboats, and will carry the guests to the house *free of charge.*   F. P. HILL.

A WINTER RESORT.
Palatka, Florida, on the St. John's River.
LARKIN HOUSE

Is an entirely new Hotel, has large rooms, high Ceilings and Perfect Ventilation; is lighted with gas; has electric Bells and Wardrobes in every room; the sleeping Rooms are handsomely furnished throughout; the table is equal to any in the country. Accommodation for 250 guests. Open December 20th, 1876.

LARKIN & MORRIS, Proprietors.

MAGNOLIA HOTEL,
ST. AUGUSTINE, FLORIDA.
W. W. PALMER, Proprietor,
Greatly repaired during the past Summer.

ST. AUGUSTINE HOTEL
St. Augustine Florida,
E. E. VAILL, Proprietor.

MARION HOUSE,
ST. AUGUSTINE, FLORIDA,
R. PALMER & CO.

BAY VIEW HOUSE,
BRUNSWICK, GA.
L. N. CLARK, Proprietor,
Of Mansion House Rockland Lake, N. Y.

St. Augustine, Florida.
First-Class Boarding Establishment,
J. L. SCOTT, Manager.

PUTNAM HOUSE,
PALATKA, FLORIDA.
F. H. ORVIS. Prop.

WINDSOR HOTEL,
JACKSONVILLE, FLORIDA.
Gould & Co., Props.

GLOBE HOTEL,
AUGUSTA, GA.
Thos. M. Binford,   John W. Cameron,
Chief Clerk.   Proprietor.

INDEX.

Historic Sketch	3
Geography	7
A Palmetto Tree. (Engraving)	9
Climate and Production	10
Thermometer Range	11
Population, Social and Political Condition	13
Florida for Pleasure Seekers	16
St. Augustine. (Engraving)	17
Florida for Invalids	19
Florida for Immigrants	22
Sketch of Charleston, S. C.	25
Sketch of Savannah, Ga.	29
Points of Interest on the Atlantic and Gulf R R	33
Points of Interest on the Florida Branch R. R.	41
Points of Interest on the Albany Branch R. R.	42
Points of Interest in Northern Florida	44
Points of Interest in Middle Florida	50
The St. John's River	56
Steamboats on St. John's River	57
Jacksonville	58
Schedule of the Steamer Hampton	62
The Attractive Points on the St. John's	62 to 69
St. Augustine	69
Fort Marion. (Engraving)	71
Western Florida	74
Southern Florida	76
Steamers to Jacksonville and Enterprise	81
Fortress Monroe, Hampton Roads, etc.	82
Aiken, S. C.	84
Wilmington, N. C.	86
Purcell House	87
How to get to Florida, (Schedules)	88
Atlantic Coast Lines	88, 89, 90
Bay Line Steamers	90
Old Dominion Steamers	91
Jacksonville to Crescent City	91
Peidmont Air Line	92
Virginia Midland Route.	93
N. Y. & Savannah Steamers	94
N. Y. & Charleston Steamers	94
Advertisements, Peidmont Air Line	95
Atlantic Coast Line Railways	96
Bay Line Steamers	97
Atlantic and Gulf Railroad	98
N. Y. and Savannah Steamers	99
The Cumberland Route	100
Old Dominion Steamship Line	101
Virginia Midland Route.	102
Atlantic and Gulf Railroad	103
Boston and New York Air Line	104
Mansion House, Fernandina	104
New Orleans, Florida & Havana S.S. Company	105
Brock & Coxetter's Line of Steamers	106
Savannah and Charleston Railroad.	106
The Magnolia Passenger Route	107
The Hygeia Hotel, Old Point Comfort, Va.	108-109
Royal Victoria Hotel, Nassau, N. P., Bahamas	110
Nassau Steamers	110
Highland Park Hotel, Aiken, S. C.	111
Atlantic Hotel, Norfolk, Va.	112
Charleston Hotel, Charleston, S C	113
Altamaha Hotel, Jesup, Ga	113
Pavilion Hotel, Charleston, S. C.	114
Marshall House, Savannah, Ga.	114
Screven House, Savannah, Ga.	115
Grand National, Jacksonville, Fla.	115
St. James' Hotel, Jacksonville, Fla.	116
Carleton House, Jacksonville, Fla.	117
Tremont House, Washington D. C.	118
Larkin House	118
Magnolia Hotel, St. Augustine	119
St. Augustine Hotel, St. Augustine.	119
Marion House, St. Augustine	119
Bay View House, Brunswick, Ga.	119
J. L. Scott, Boarding Establishment.	119
Putman House, Palatka, Fla	119
Windsor Hotel, Jacksonville, Fla.	119
Globe Hotel, Augusta, Ga.	119

www.ingramcontent.com/pod-product-compliance
Lightning Source LLC
Chambersburg PA
CBHW021942160426
43195CB00011B/1187